More cookbooks by Natalie Aul

- Weight Loss Recipes Cookbook Volumes 1-13
- Cooking with Joy
- Cooking with Joy 2
- Weight Loss Recipes Cookbook Whole Food, Plant Based, & Vegan Volume
- Weight Loss Recipes Cookbook Whole Food, Plant Based, & Vegan Volume 2
- Simply Delicious A 14 Day Food Plan
- Weight Loss Recipes Cookbook Holiday Volume

Special Thanks to:
My sister Kelly, without you this book would not be possible!
My mom Maggie, for your encouragement, and introducing us to this new way of life.
To everyone who has sent me encouraging notes and such lovely reviews of my other cookbook
volumes, you have all been so sweet!
And to YOU my recipe family who keeps me inspired and drooling daily.
I give all the glory to God, without Him I can do nothing. He is my guide and inspiration for each of
these recipes. He is my encourager to keep reach my goals and beyond!

"Blessed are the pure in heart for they shall see God."
Matthew 5:8

RECIPE CONTENTS

Breakfast

1. 5 Grain Porridge
2. Peanut Butter Blueberry Muffins
3. Banana Nut Bars
4. Frosted Pumpkin Muffins
5. Pumpkin Nut Muffins
6. Berries and Crème Bars
7. Pumpkin Cottage Squares
8. Orange Walnut Bars
9. Blueberry Nutter Butter Muffins
10. PB&J Pie
11. Peach Walnut Cake
12. Lemon Blueberry Cottage Cake
13. Blueberry Cottage Cake with Oat Crust
14. Blueberry Nut Tops
15. Strawberry Banana Baked Oatmeal
16. Strawberry Banana Muffies
17. Berry Blondie Muffies
18. Batch Steel Cut Oats
19. Steel Cut Overnight Oats
20. French Toast Casserole
21. Cheesy Ranch Taters
22. Crispy Seasoned Potatoes
23. Chipotle Potato wedges
24. Chipotle Air Fried Crispy Potatoes
25. Potato Crisps
26. Berry Baked Oatmeal
27. PB&J Crisp
28. Potato Crust Quiche
29. Fiesta Potato Quiche

Lunch

31. Who am I now?"
34. Mango Cheesecake Bars
35. Chicken Vegetable Frittata
36. Creamy Tuna Bowl
37. Cheesecake Lentil Berry Bars
38. Turkey Stuffing Muffies
39. Blueberry Goat Cheese Scones
40. Tuna Casserole Bars
41. Coconut Berry Bars
42. Peach Cheddar Bars
43. Blueberry Chia Bars
44. Gingerbread Pecan Blondies
45. Green Bean Quiche
46. Asian Scrabble Stir Fry
47. Pumpkin Nut Cheesecake Bars
48. Spinach Tuna Melt
49. Blueberry Blondie Muffies
50. Ricotta Gnocchi
51. Spinach Apple Fritters
52. Fruity Chia Bars
53. Tuna Cakes

Dinner

55. "Shock Your Brain"
59. Asian Stir Fry Batch Cook
60. Oriental Stir Fry Bowl
61. Green Bean Soup
62. Bacon Vegetable Lasagna
63. Lasagna Bowl
64. Creamy Vegetables Chowder

65. Squash Chili
66. Pizza Lasagna
67. Enchilada Casserole
68. Butter Nut Squash Casserole
69. Oriental Casserole
70. Mushroom Squash Swiss
71. Turkey Dinner Soup
72. Cheeseburger Pizza Bowl
73. Thanksgiving Leftover Casserole
74. Thankful Turkey Chowder
75. Tomato Soup and Grilled Cheese
76. Cheesy Turkey Casserole
77. Vegetable Beef Soup
78. Creamy Tuscan Chicken Noodle Soup
79. Vegan Cheesy Artichoke Palmini Pasta Bowl with Rosemary Balsamic Fried Chicken
80. Turkey Burger Bowl
81. Shepherd's Pie
82. Lasagna Casserole
83. Crispy Pizza Casserole
84. Cheesy Green Bean Casserole
85. Cordon Blue Vegetable Lasagna
86. Ranch Queichearole
87. Tuscan Pizza Casserole
88. Cheesy Tomato Soup
89. Chicken Noodle Soup
90. Slow Cooker Cabbage Lasagna
91. Skinny Shepherd's Pie
92. Cheeseburger Soup
93. Tuscan Onion Soup
94. The BEST Pot Roast
95. Instapot Pot Roast
96. Taco Ricotta Casserole
97. Broccoli Cheese Soup
98. Taco Supreme Casserole
99. Tex-mex Casserole
100. Chicken Chili
101.Bean Less Chili
102. Chili
103. Vegetable Lasagna Soup
104. Beef Stroganoff
105. Red Bean Thai Peanut Bowl

Sauces, Seasonings, and Sides

106. Enchilada sauce
107. Ranch Mockoritos
108. Dijon Lemon Dipping Sauce
109. Cranberry Pineapple Jam
110. Orange Cranberry Jam
111. Homemade Salsa
112. Avocado Fries
113. Homemade Tomato Sauce
114. Berry Rhubarb Jam
115. Pineapple Rhubarb Jam
116. Fat Free Pesto

Vegetables

117. Baked Zucchini
118. Basil Refrigerator Pickles
119. Air Fried Crispy Onions
120. Air Fryer Zucchini Fries
121. Air Fried Radish Taters
122. Crispy Air Fried Cabbage
123. Chipotle Eggplant Fries
124. Cauli Rice Veggie Wok
125. Parsnip Air Fryer Cheesy Fries
126. Crispy Hot Cauli Wings
127. BBQ Air Fryer Cauliflower
128. Cinnamon Refried Squash
129. Air Fryer Carrot Chips
130. Carrot Buffalo Crisps
131. Buffalo Eggplant Fries
132. Fried Zucchini
133. Cinnamon Air Fried Carrot Crisps
134. Ginger Curry Stir Fry
135. Cauliflower Ranch Stir Fry
136. Cheese Less Cheesy Carrot Fries

137. Creamy Cauliflower Mashed Potatoes
138. Cheese Less Cheesy Cabbage
139. Ranch Roasted Cauliflower Bites
140. Cheesy Roasted Radishes
141. Tomato Basil Carrot Fries
142. Zucchini Chips
143. Chili Cheese Carrot Fries
144. Asian Air Fried Salad
145. Cheesy Air Fried Green Tomatoes
146. Air Fried Mushrooms
147. Garlic Balsamic Roasted Mushrooms
148. Crispy Squash Chips
149. Asian Roasted Cabbage
150. Balsamic Rosemary Roasted Radish Taters
151. Grilled Seasoned Vegetables
152. Grilled Vegetables
153. Garlic Dill Refrigerator Cucumbers

Fruits

154. Crockpot Apples and Spice
155. Cinnamon Air Fried Fruit
156. Coffee Air Fried Apples and Banana
157. Air Fried Grapes
158. Cinnamon Air Fried Apples

Meats & Protein

160. Cheesy Chicken Nuggets
161. Rosemary Balsamic Fried Chicken
162. Seasoned Grilled Chicken
163. Air Fryer Roasted Chickpeas
164. Sea Salt Vinegar Air Fried Chickpeas
165. Chipotle Air Fried Chickpeas
166. 2 Ingredient Lentil Tortillas
167. Lentil Flatbread
168. Lentil Flatbread Crisps
169. Ginger Cumin Chicken
170. Chili Lime Chicken

171. Pressure Cooker Seasoned Chicken
172. Savory Lentil Wraps
173. Sweet Lentil Wraps
174. Lentil Pizzelle
175. Oriental Chicken
176. Marinated Tuna Steak
177. Grilled Pesto Chicken
178. Fat Free Hummus
179. Golden Hummus
180. Pesto Hummus

Party Servings

181. Peanut Asian Noodle Salad
182. Party Peanut Butter Frosted Apple Crisp
183. 4th of July Party Salad
184. Cheesecake Berry Salad

Seasonings

185. Chipotle Seasoning
186. Gingerbread spice
187. Ranch Seasoning
188. Oriental Seasoning
189. Pumpkin Pie Spice
190. Apple Pie Spice
191. Greek Spice Blend
192. Latte Spice
193. Chai spice
194. Hash Seasoning
195. Seasoned Fry Spice
196. Taco Seasoning

Breakfast

1 GRAIN, 1 PROTEIN, 6OZ FRUIT

Food addiction is not like other addictions. Most addictions you can stop cold turkey, but you can't exactly do that with food. Most diets fail, are not realistic, or are not sustainable. "Run 20 miles, do 30 burpee's, then hike Mount Everest. You will be skinny in no time!" or "Eat our pre-made food… it tastes like cardboard and you will be starving most of the time." Or "Eat only baked fish and broccoli" or "Take these pills and drink this potion and BAM thin!" These yo-yo diets do not deal with the real problem and you can't live on pills or climb Mount Everest forever… so the weight comes back.

What if I told you there was a better way to lose weight, be healthy, and keep the weight off? You even get to eat a lot of delicious food without starving the whole time! If I can do it, a chunky kid who loved pizza, ice cream, and mac & cheese, you can do it! I will give you all the recipes (that's the hard part).

Sugar free, flour free, 3 weighed meals a day (no snacks in between). Deliciously FREE!

With Joy, Natalie

"Look at me. I stand at the door. I knock. If you hear me call and open the door, I'll come right in and sit down to supper with you. Conquerors will sit alongside me at the head table, just as I, having conquered, took the place of honor at the side of my Father. That's my gift to the conquerors!2 Revelation 3:20-21 MSG

Weight loss Recipes
- no sugar, no flour, made deliciously easy -
WeightLossRecipesCookbook.com

5 Grain Porridge

servings: 5   cooking time: 30 min

INGREDIENTS

- 1oz of each: Steel cut oats, wheat berries, amaranth, quinoa, grits
- 25oz Water

DIRECTIONS

1. Add all ingredients to an instant pot and pressure cook on high 20min.
2. Natural release 5min then quick release.
3. Or add all ingredients to a pot and bring to a boil.
4. Reduce heat and cover.
5. Simmer 30-40min or until mixture is thickened.
6. Divide into 5 separate servings.

SIDE EACH SERVING WITH:
6oz fruit and a protein for a complete breakfast.
Add 2-3Tbsp of water to porridge and mix for reheating.

Peanut Butter Blueberry Muffins

servings: 4   cooking time: 30 min

INGREDIENTS

- 4oz Uncooked oats (full grain)
- 1tsp of each: Baking soda, baking powder, vanilla extract
- 12oz Banana (1/2 fruit)
- 12oz Frozen blueberries (1/2 fruit)
- 4 Eggs (1/2 protein)
- 2oz Peanut butter (1/4 protein)
- 1oz Walnuts (1/8 protein)
- 4oz Plain Greek yogurt (1/8 protein)
- Pinch of Sea salt

DIRECTIONS

1. Preheat oven to 350.
2. Line 2 muffins pans (24 muffins) with silicone liners or lightly oil pans.
3. Add all ingredients to a large bowl and mash/mix.
4. Divide mixture into muffin pans and bake 30min.

SERVING SIZE:
6 Muffins = 1 full breakfast serving

Weight loss Recipes
- no sugar, no flour, made deliciously easy -
WeightLossRecipesCookbook.com

3

Banana Nut Bars

servings: 4   cooking time: 30 min

INGREDIENTS

- 24oz Banana (full fruit)
- 4 Eggs (1/2 protein)
- 2oz Walnuts (1/4 protein)
- 2oz Peanut butter (1/4 protein)
- 4oz Uncooked oats (full grain)
- 1tsp of each: Baking soda, baking powder, vanilla extract
- Pinch of Sea salt

DIRECTIONS

1. Preheat oven to 350.
2. Add all ingredients to a large bowl and mash/mix.
3. Lightly oil a bar pan or a muffin pan.
4. Divide mixture into 36 bars and bake 30min.

SERVING SIZE:
9 Bars = 1 full breakfast serving

Frosted Pumpkin Muffins

servings: 4   cooking time: 30 min

INGREDIENTS

- 3 Eggs
- 2oz Peanut butter
- 3oz Canned chickpeas
- 4oz Plain Greek yogurt
- 1oz Walnuts
- 12oz Banana
- 12oz Canned pumpkin
- 1Tbsp of each: Pumpkin pie spice, vanilla extract
- 1tsp of each: Baking soda, baking powder
- Pinch of Sea salt
- 4oz Uncooked oats

DIRECTIONS

1. Preheat oven to 350.
2. Add all ingredients except 1oz peanut butter and yogurt to a large bowl and mix.
3. Lightly oil 2 12 muffin, muffin pans.
4. Divide mixture into 20 muffins.
5. Bake 25-30min or until a toothpick comes out clean.
6. In a separate bowl mix yogurt and 1oz peanut butter.
7. Top muffins with yogurt mixture.

SERVING SIZE:
5 Muffins = 1 full breakfast serving

Weight loss Recipes
- no sugar, no flour, made deliciously easy -
WeightLossRecipesCookbook.com

Pumpkin Nut Muffins

servings: 4   cooking time: 30 min

INGREDIENTS

- 4oz Uncooked oats
- 12oz of each: Banana, canned pumpkin
- 4oz total: Peanut butter, walnuts
- 2tsp Pumpkin Pie Spice
- 1/2tsp of each: Baking soda, baking powder
- 1tsp Almond extract
- 4 Eggs
- Pinch of Sea salt

DIRECTIONS

1. Preheat oven to 375.
2. Add all ingredients to a large bowl and mash/mix.
3. Line 2 12 muffin pans.
4. Divide mixture into muffins and bake 30min.

SERVING SIZE:
6 Muffins = 1 full breakfast serving

Weight loss Recipes
- no sugar, no flour, made deliciously easy -
WeightLossRecipesCookbook.com

Berries and Crème Bars

servings: 4   cooking time: 60 min

INGREDIENTS

- 4oz Uncooked oats
- 12oz Banana
- 12oz Mixed berries (blueberries, cherries, strawberries, raspberries)
- 1/2tsp of each: Baking soda, baking powder
- Pinch of Sea salt
- 1Tbsp Vanilla extract
- 4 Eggs
- 8oz Cottage cheese

DIRECTIONS

1. Preheat oven to 375.
2. Add all ingredients to a large bowl and mash/mix.
3. Lightly oil a 9x13 cake pan.
4. Pour batter into pan and bake 35-40min or until center is set.
5. Let cool 10min before dividing into 4 servings.

Weight loss Recipes
- no sugar, no flour, made deliciously easy -
WeightLossRecipesCookbook.com

Pumpkin Cottage Squares

servings: 3   cooking time: 30 min

INGREDIENTS

- 9oz Canned pumpkin
- 9oz Banana
- 3oz Uncooked oats
- 3 Eggs
- 6oz Cottage cheese
- 1Tbsp Pumpkin pie spice
- 2tsp Vanilla extract
- Pinch of Sea salt

DIRECTIONS

1. Preheat oven to 350.
2. Lightly oil a bar pan, donut pan, or muffin pan.
3. Divide batter into 18 bars and bake 30min.

SERVING SIZE:
6 Bars = 1 full breakfast serving

Weight loss Recipes

- no sugar, no flour, made deliciously easy -

WeightLossRecipesCookbook.com

Orange Walnut Bars

servings: 4   cooking time: 30 min

INGREDIENTS

- 12oz Banana
- 12oz Orange (about 3 oranges)
- 4oz Uncooked oats
- 4 Eggs
- 4oz Walnuts
- 1tsp of each: Baking soda, cinnamon, almond extract
- Pinch of Sea salt

DIRECTIONS

1. Preheat oven to 350.
2. Mash banana.
3. Add eggs, baking soda, seasonings, oats, and mix.
4. Line a baking pan or cake pan with parchment paper.
5. Scoop mixture into pan.
6. Zest one orange and sprinkle on pan.
7. Slice oranges into pieces.
8. Sprinkle bake with walnuts and orange slices. Bake 30min.

SERVING SIZE:
Divide into 4 portions.

Weight loss Recipes
- no sugar, no flour, made deliciously easy -
WeightLossRecipesCookbook.com

Blueberry Nutter Butter Muffins

servings: 3   cooking time: 30 min

INGREDIENTS

- 12oz Banana
- 6oz Frozen blueberries
- 3oz Uncooked oats
- 3 Eggs
- 2oz Plain Greek yogurt
- 1oz Walnuts
- 1 1/2oz Peanut butter
- 1tsp of each: Almond extract, cinnamon
- 3/4tsp of each: Baking soda, baking powder
- Pinch of Sea salt

DIRECTIONS

1. Preheat oven to 350.
2. Line a muffin pan or lightly oil a muffin pan.
3. Add all ingredients to a large bowl and mash/mix.
4. Divide mixture into 18 muffins. Bake 30min.

SERVING SIZE:
6 Muffins = 1 full breakfast serving

Weight loss Recipes
- no sugar, no flour, made deliciously easy -
WeightLossRecipesCookbook.com

PB&J Pie

servings: 3   cooking time: 40 min

INGREDIENTS

- 10oz Banana
- 8oz Frozen mixed berries (blueberries, strawberries, raspberries, cherries)
- 3 Eggs
- 3oz Peanut butter
- Pinch of each: Sea salt, cinnamon, vanilla extract
- 3oz Uncooked oats

DIRECTIONS

1. Preheat oven to 375.
2. Add all ingredients except berries to a large bowl and mash/mix.
3. Lightly oil a pie dish.
4. Scoop mixture into pie dish and top with berries
5. Bake 35-40min.
6. Cut pie into 6 slices

SERVING SIZE:
2 slices = 1 full breakfast serving

Weight loss Recipes
- no sugar, no flour, made deliciously easy -
WeightLossRecipesCookbook.com

Peach Walnut Cake

servings: 3   cooking time: 30 min

INGREDIENTS

- 10oz Banana
- 8oz Peaches
- 3oz Uncooked oats
- 1/2tsp of each: Baking soda, baking powder, vanilla extract
- 3 Eggs
- 2tsp Cinnamon
- 3oz Walnuts

DIRECTIONS

1. Preheat oven to 375.
2. Lightly oil a medium cake pan or baking dish.
3. Add all ingredients except peaches and cinnamon to a large bowl and mash/mix.
4. Pour mixture into cake pan and top with peaches and sprinkle with cinnamon.
5. Bake 30min.
6. Cut Cake into 6 slices

SERVING SIZE:
2 slices = 1 full breakfast serving

Weight loss Recipes
- no sugar, no flour, made deliciously easy -
WeightLossRecipesCookbook.com

Lemon Blueberry Cottage Cake

servings: 4   cooking time: 30 min

INGREDIENTS

- 8oz Cottage cheese
- 1tsp Lemon extract
- 2Tbsp Lemon juice
- 4oz Uncooked oats
- 18oz Banana
- 6oz Frozen blueberries
- 1/2tsp of each: Baking soda, baking powder
- 4 Eggs

DIRECTIONS

1. Preheat oven to 375.
2. Mash banana.
3. Add all ingredients to a large bowl and mix.
4. Lightly oil a large baking dish or cake pan.
5. Pour mixture into baking dish and bake 30min.
6. Let cool 10min before dividing into 4 servings

SERVING SIZE:
1/4th of cake = 1 full breakfast serving

Weight loss Recipes
- no sugar, no flour, made deliciously easy -
WeightLossRecipesCookbook.com

Blueberry Cottage Cake with Oat Crust

servings: 4   cooking time: 30 min

INGREDIENTS

- 4oz Uncooked oats
- 16oz Banana
- 8oz Frozen blueberries
- 2tsp Vanilla extract
- 4 Eggs
- 8oz Cottage cheese
- Pinch of Sea salt

DIRECTIONS

1. Preheat oven to 375.
2. Slice banana.
3. Add remaining ingredients except oats to sliced banana and mix.
4. Lightly oil a med/large baking dish and sprinkle with oats.
5. Top oats with banana mixture and gently spread until even.
6. Bake 30min.
7. Let cool 10min before dividing into 4 servings

SERVING SIZE:
1/4th of cake = 1 full breakfast serving

Weight loss Recipes
- no sugar, no flour, made deliciously easy -
WeightLossRecipesCookbook.com

Blueberry Nut Tops

servings: 3   cooking time: 30 min

INGREDIENTS

- 3oz Canned chickpeas
- 2 1/2oz Peanut butter
- 2 1/2oz Walnuts
- 1/2tsp Baking soda
- 3oz Uncooked oats
- 14oz Banana
- 4oz Frozen blueberries
- 1tsp of each: Cinnamon, vanilla extract
- Pinch of Sea salt

DIRECTIONS

1. Preheat oven to 350.
2. Drain and blend chickpeas with a hand blender or food processor until smooth.
3. Add banana, oats, cinnamon, vanilla, salt, baking soda, peanut butter, and mash/mix.
4. Add remaining ingredients and mix.
5. Line a baking pan with parchment paper.
6. Dollop mixture into 12 cookies onto the baking pan
7. Bake 30min.

SERVING SIZE:
4 Cookies = 1 full breakfast serving

Weight loss Recipes
- no sugar, no flour, made deliciously easy -
WeightLossRecipesCookbook.com

Strawberry Banana Baked Oatmeal

servings: 4   cooking time: 40min

INGREDIENTS

- 4oz Whole milk
- 4 Eggs
- 4oz Uncooked oats
- Pinch of Sea salt
- 24oz total frozen or fresh: strawberries, banana
- 3oz Peanut butter
- 1tsp Vanilla extract

DIRECTIONS

1. Preheat oven to 350.
2. Mix oats, milk, eggs, salt, and vanilla.
3. Add fruit to oat mixture and mix.
4. Lightly oil a 9x9 baking dish.
5. Pour mixture into dish and drizzle with peanut butter.
6. Bake 35min. Let cool 10min before dividing into 4 servings.

SERVING SIZE:
1/4th of cake = 1 full breakfast serving

Strawberry Banana Muffies

servings: 4   cooking time. 35min

INGREDIENTS

- 24oz total frozen: Strawberries and bananas
- 4 Eggs
- 2oz Walnuts (or your favorite nuts)
- 2oz Peanut butter (or your favorite nut butter)
- 1tsp of each: Baking soda, baking powder, strawberry extract or vanilla extract
- Pinch of Sea salt
- 4oz Uncooked oats

DIRECTIONS

1. Preheat oven to 375.
2. Add all ingredients to a large bowl except fruit and mix.
3. Add fruit (if using fresh banana, slice first) to bowl and mix.
4. Line or lightly oil 2 12 muffin, muffin pans.
5. Divide mixture into each muffin making sure to get at least 1 strawberry and 1 banana slice in each one.
6. Bake 35min.

SERVING SIZE:
6 muffins = 1 full breakfast serving

Weight loss Recipes
- no sugar, no flour, made deliciously easy -
WeightLossRecipesCookbook.com

Berry Blondie Muffies

servings: 4   cooking time: 30min

INGREDIENTS

- 18oz Banana
- 6oz Frozen berries (blueberries, cherries)
- 9oz Canned chickpeas
- 1/2oz each: Ground flax seed, chia seeds
- 2oz Almond butter (or your favorite nut butter)
- 2oz Walnuts (or your favorite nuts)
- 2oz Uncooked oats
- 2oz Uncooked amaranth (or do 4oz total of oats)
- 2tsp Cinnamon
- 1tsp of each: Nutmeg, vanilla extract, almond extract, baking soda, baking powder.

DIRECTIONS

1. Preheat oven to 375.
2. Lightly oil 2 muffin pans or bar pans.
3. Drain and blend chickpeas with a hand blender or food processor until smooth.
4. Mash banana.
5. Add all ingredients to a large bowl and mix.
6. Divide mixture into muffin pans and bake 30min.
7. Divide into 4 separate servings.

SERVING SIZE:
1/4th of muffins = 1 full breakfast serving

Weight loss Recipes
- no sugar, no flour, made deliciously easy -
WeightLossRecipesCookbook.com

Batch Steel Cut Oats

servings: 4   cooking time: 45min

INGREDIENTS

- 4oz Uncooked steel cut oats (full grain)
- 4 Cups water
- 1/4tsp Sea salt

DIRECTIONS

1. Add water to a medium pot.
2. Bring to a boil.
3. Stir in oats and reduce heat to low/med.
4. Simmer 20-30min or until desired consistency.
5. Remove from heat and let cool 5-10min.
6. Divide oats into 4 separate servings.
7. In the morning add cooked oats and 2Tbsp water to a bowl.
8. Microwave or heat on the stovetop.
9. Add desired protein/toppings, and fruit.

SERVING SIZE:
1/4th cooked oats = 1 full grain serving

Weight loss Recipes
- no sugar, no flour, made deliciously easy -
WeightLossRecipesCookbook.com

Steel Cut Overnight Oats

servings: 8   cooking time: 10min

INGREDIENTS

- 1cup Steel cut oats
- 3cups Water
- Pinch of Sea salt

DIRECTIONS

1. Add oats and salt to a medium pot and heat over med/low heat.
2. Toast oats 4-5min or until golden brown and fragrant.
3. Add water.
4. Increase heat to high and bring to a boil.
5. Remove from heat, cover, and let sit overnight.
6. In the morning scoop 4oz into a bowl and add desired toppings.

SERVING SIZE:
4oz cooked = full grain

Weight loss Recipes
- no sugar, no flour, made deliciously easy -
WeightLossRecipesCookbook.com

French Toast Casserole

servings: 6   cooking time: 1hr 20min

INGREDIENTS

- 6 Slices Ezekiel bread (full grain)
- 6 Eggs (1/2 protein)
- 6oz Milk (1/8 protein)
- 6oz Plain Greek yogurt (1/8 protein)
- 2lb 3oz total: Frozen berries (blueberries, cherries, raspberries), banana (full fruit)
- 1Tbsp of each: Cinnamon, vanilla extract
- 1tsp Baking soda
- 1/2tsp of each: Sea salt, nutmeg

DIRECTIONS

1. Lightly oil a large baking dish or a 9x13 cake pan.
2. Add bread slices to baking dish.
3. Whisk eggs, milk, yogurt, and seasonings.
4. Pour egg mixture over bread slices.
5. Flip bread. Let soak 20min.
6. Preheat oven to 375.
7. Slice bananas.
8. Top bread slices with fruits.
9. Bake 50-60min or until eggs are set.
10. Divide casserole into 6 slices.
11. Top with ¼ protein for a complete breakfast.

SERVING SIZE:
1/6th of casserole = full breakfast

Weight loss Recipes
- no sugar, no flour, made deliciously easy -
WeightLossRecipesCookbook.com

Cheesy Ranch Taters

servings: -   cooking time- 25min

INGREDIENTS

- 3-4 Potatoes
- 1Tbsp of each: Nutritional yeast, ranch seasoning
- Pinch of Sea salt

DIRECTIONS

1. Dice potatoes into small pieces.
2. Add potatoes and seasoning to a bowl and mix.
3. Line an air fryer with parchment paper.
4. Add potatoes and cook 400 for 25min.
5. Stir halfway for even roasting.
6. Or bake 375 for 40-45min stirring halfway.

SINGLE SERVING SIZE-
4oz = full grain

Weight loss Recipes
- no sugar, no flour, made deliciously easy -
WeightLossRecipesCookbook.com

Crispy Seasoned Potatoes

servings: -   cooking time- 25min

INGREDIENTS

- 1-3 Raw potatoes
- 1Tbsp of each: Season fry seasoning, nutritional yeast
- Pinch of Sea salt

DIRECTIONS

1. Dice potatoes into small pieces.
2. Add seasonings and toss to evenly coat.
3. Line an air fryer with parchment paper or use a pan that will fit in the air fryer.
4. Air fry at 400 for 25min.
5. Stir halfway for even roasting.
6. or bake 375 for 40min stirring occasionally for even roasting.

SINGLE SERVING SIZE-
4oz = full grain

Weight loss Recipes

- no sugar, no flour, made deliciously easy -

WeightLossRecipesCookbook.com

23

Chipotle Potato wedges

servings: -   cooking time: 40min

INGREDIENTS

- 1-3 Potatoes
- Chipotle seasoning
- Spray olive oil

DIRECTIONS

1. Preheat oven to 375 or use an air fryer.
2. Cut potatoes into wedges or matchsticks.
3. Lightly spray with olive oil, sprinkle with seasoning, and toss to coat.
4. Lightly oil a baking pan or place potatoes in an air fryer and fry 390 for 35-40min or until desired crispiness, stir every 10-15min for even cooking or bake 35-40min.

SINGLE SERVING SIZE-
4oz = full grain

Weight loss Recipes
- no sugar, no flour, made deliciously easy -
WeightLossRecipesCookbook.com

24

Chipotle Air Fried Crispy Potatoes

servings: -   cooking time: 40min

INGREDIENTS

- 1-3 Potatoes
- Chipotle seasoning
- Spray olive oil

DIRECTIONS

1. Slice potatoes thin.
2. Lightly spray with olive oil.
3. Sprinkle with seasoning.
4. Place potatoes in an air fryer and cook 390 for 25min.
5. Stir and cook another 10-15min or until desired crispiness.

SINGLE SERVING SIZE-
4oz = full grain

Weight loss Recipes
- no sugar, no flour, made deliciously easy -
WeightLossRecipesCookbook.com

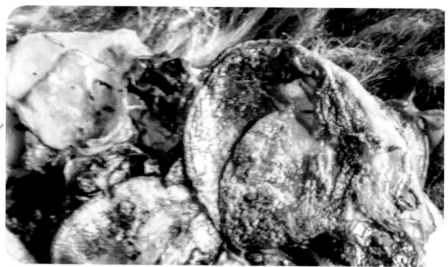

Potato Crisps

servings: -   cooking time: 25min

INGREDIENTS

- Potatoes
- Sea salt

DIRECTIONS

1. Preheat oven to 400.
2. Lightly oil a baking sheet.
3. Slice potatoes thin.
4. Sprinkle with sea salt and bake.
5. Toss/flip every 5min until potatoes are a golden brown.

Find this recipe also in my Volume 3 cookbook and Cooking with Joy.

SINGLE SERVING SIZE-
4oz = full grain

Weight loss Recipes
- no sugar, no flour, made deliciously easy -
WeightLossRecipesCookbook.com

Berry Baked Oatmeal

servings: 4   cooking time: 35min

INGREDIENTS

- 12oz Banana
- 12oz Berries
- 4oz Uncooked oats
- 1 1/2oz Chia seeds
- 8oz Milk
- 2 Eggs
- 1 1/2oz Peanut butter
- 2oz Cottage cheese
- 1/2tsp Baking soda, sea salt, vanilla extract

DIRECTIONS

1. Preheat oven to 375.
2. Slice banana.
3. Place fruit in the bottom of a medium baking dish.
4. Sprinkle fruit with oats. In a separate bowl mix milk, cottage cheese, eggs, chia seeds, baking soda, salt, and vanilla.
5. Pour mixture onto baking dish and drizzle with peanut butter.
6. Bake 30-35min.
7. Divide into 4.

SINGLE SERVING SIZE-
1/4th of bake = full breakfast

Weight loss Recipes
- no sugar, no flour, made deliciously easy -
WeightLossRecipesCookbook.com

PB&J Crisp

servings: 3   cooking time: 45min

INGREDIENTS
- 2oz Peanut butter
- 2oz Walnuts
- 8oz Milk
- 3oz Uncooked oats
- 9oz Banana
- 9oz Frozen berries (cherries, blueberries, strawberries)
- 1tsp of each: Cinnamon, vanilla extract
- Pinch of Sea salt

DIRECTIONS
1. Preheat oven to 375.
2. Slice banana.
3. Add fruit to a medium baking dish.
4. In a separate bowl mix remaining ingredients.
5. Pour mixture onto fruit.
6. Bake 45min.
7. Divide into 3 servings.

SINGLE SERVING SIZE-
1/3th of bake = full breakfast

Weight loss Recipes
- no sugar, no flour, made deliciously easy -
WeightLossRecipesCookbook.com

Potato Crust Quiche

servings: 4   cooking time: 1hr 30min

INGREDIENTS

- 20oz Raw potatoes (will shrink when cooked)
- 4 Eggs
- 8oz Cottage cheese
- 2Tbsp Season fry seasoning
- 12oz Frozen green beans
- 12oz Frozen corn

DIRECTIONS

1. Preheat oven to 375.
2. Line or lightly oil a 9x13 cake pan.
3. Cut potatoes into slices.
4. Layer potatoes in the bottom of the cake pan.
5. Mix eggs, seasonings, and cottage cheese.
6. Add frozen veggies to egg mixture and mix.
7. Pour mixture on top of potatoes.
8. Bake 1hr 30min or until potatoes are tender and egg mixture is set and no longer glossy.
9. Cut and divide into 4 servings

SINGLE SERVING SIZE-
1/4th of quiche = full breakfast

29

Weight loss Recipes
- no sugar, no flour, made deliciously easy -
WeightLossRecipesCookbook.com

Fiesta Potato Quiche

servings: 3   cooking time: 1hr

INGREDIENTS

- 3 Eggs
- 3oz Shredded cheese
- 15oz Potatoes
- 6oz Frozen or canned corn
- 12oz Frozen California blend (cauliflower, broccoli, carrots)
- 1Tbsp Taco seasoning

DIRECTIONS

1. Preheat oven to 375.
2. Lightly oil a large pie dish.
3. Dice potatoes into small pieces.
4. Mix potatoes, eggs, cheese, and seasoning.
5. Pour vegetables into pie dish.
6. Pour potato mixture on top of veggies.
7. Bake 1hr or until potatoes are tender.
8. Divide pie into 3 servings

SINGLE SERVING SIZE-
1/3th of quiche = full breakfast

Lunch

1 PROTEIN, 1 FAT, 6OZ VEGETABLES, 6OZ FRUIT

"Who am I now?"

When I made the decision to cut out sugar, flour, and only eat three meals a day, it felt like I died. I literally went through a grieving process over food! After that grieving, I felt like I didn't know who I was.

We go through seasons of changes where we transform into something new just like caterpillars. When a caterpillar enters that chrysalis, it turns into a liquid substance. Sometimes life can feel like this, we feel like a puddle of goo. But if you trust the process and keep at it, you will start forming your new identity. You will then break out of that chrysalis and become something completely new and beautiful!

What do you do when you are in the "goo" phase? Cling and hold on even tighter to the food plan, the process, and God.

The footnotes to 2 Cor. 17-18 TPT are amazing!
 *"This would include our old identity, our life of sin (or overeating and food bondage), the religious works of trying to please God, our old relationship with the world (and food), and our old mindsets. We are not reformed or simply refurbished, we are made completely new by our union with Christ and the indwelling of the Holy Spirit."
 **"Who has restored us to friendship with God."

Now, if anyone is enfolded into Christ, he has become an entirely new person. All that is related to the old order has vanished. Behold everything is fresh and new. And God has made all things new, and reconciled** us to Himself, and given us the ministry of reconciling others to God.*
2 Corinthians 5:17-18 TPT

When we trust the metamorphosis process and trust God, He doesn't just refurbish us. He makes us COMPLETELY BRAND NEW!

One translation says, *"A new species that has never existed before."* Those old bad habits, thinking, desires, and cravings have all been put to death.

The footnote to Galatians 5:24 TPT says, *"All our fleshly passions and desires"* includes cravings! But you might be thinking, "I'm still craving those things!" Our soul (mind, will, and emotions) need to be renewed daily. How do we do that? By filling our minds with the transforming Word of God.

Before it goes into that chrysalis, that caterpillar will eat and eat and eat and fill itself so full of food because it knows it's going to need that fuel during its transformation. It's the same with us. We can feed and feed and feed our minds with healing, transforming, powerful words of truth from God. It energizes, comforts, and gives us such peace. These days it's so easy to do. We have apps, the internet, books, music, and so much more. I have a podcast app on my phone with powerful faith preaching that I have playing every chance I get. I have worship music at the tips of my fingers. I can search peace, joy, or whatever I need at the moment and find scripture on the internet. I have positive affirmations on my treadmill, on my bathroom mirror, next to my bed. I say those. That's transforming and forming new habits, cravings, and a new mindset to live FREE!

Keep in mind that we who belong to Jesus Christ have already experienced crucifixion. For everything connected to our self-life* was put to death on the cross and crucified with Messiah. If the Spirit is the source of our life, we must also allow the Spirit to direct every aspect of our lives. Galatians 5:24-25 TPT

AFFIRMATIONS BY MY BED

Transformation isn't just a one-time event. It is a daily process. It's easier to maintain things daily than trying to do a complete overhaul once a month. Just like brushing your teeth, it's easier to do it 2x a day than to do nothing and only have the dentist clean them off once every six months. You would most likely lose some teeth and have major decay if you did it this way.

It's the same with us. We can start experiencing "truth decay." When this happens we need to "brush up" on the truth. The truth is, we are free, we are new creations, the old habits and cravings have been crucified with our old self-life. We need to remind ourselves of these truths in the easy times and especially in the hard times. Transformation is a process, its a journey, but in the end all the little daily decisions and choices add up to big victories and progress! Those choices and decisions are worth it every time.

Pray this with me "Father God, I make the choice to trust you to transform me. I am willing to change, to change my thinking, to change my habits, and to change my life. I trust you to lead me in the steps I need to take to transform the habits I need to get rid of, and the new habits I need to create. I trust you in this daily transformation process and I trust you with my life. In Jesus name, Amen."

Some affirmation ideas:
I am in the best shape of my life.
I am fit, firm, and strong.
I have a healthy and strong metabolism.
My mind and body are at peace with food.
I am loved, I am at peace, I have joy.
I am kind, loving, content, and thankful.
Everyday and in everyway I am getting better and better because of my covenant with God.
I have the greater One in me who puts me over in life.
I am easily led and guided by the Holy Spirit in every decision in life.

WITH JOY,

Natalie

Weight loss Recipes
- no sugar, no flour, made deliciously easy -
WeightLossRecipesCookbook.com

Mango Cheesecake Bars

servings: 4   cooking time: 30 min

INGREDIENTS

- 4 Eggs
- 12oz Banana
- 12oz Frozen mango
- 2tsp Vanilla extract
- Pinch of Sea salt
- 1oz Peanut butter or tahini
- 1oz Walnuts
- 2oz Ricotta cheese
- 4oz Plain Greek yogurt

DIRECTIONS

1. Preheat oven to 350.
2. Add all ingredients to a large bowl and mash/mix.
3. Lightly oil 4 small baking dishes.
4. Divide mixture into baking dishes and bake 30min.
5. Refrigerate 4hrs-overnight before eating.

SIDE EACH SERVING WITH:
6oz vegetables and a fat for a complete lunch.

Weight loss Recipes
- no sugar, no flour, made deliciously easy -
WeightLossRecipesCookbook.com

Chicken Vegetable Frittata

servings: 4   cooking time: 45 min

INGREDIENTS

- 24oz total frozen: Mixed vegetables, peppers, onions
- 8oz total: Cooked or canned chicken, ricotta cheese
- 4 Eggs
- 4oz Shredded cheese
- 1/2tsp Baking soda
- 1Tbsp Seasoned fry seasoning (Find this seasoning in "Sauces, Seasonings, and Sides")

DIRECTIONS

1. Preheat oven to 375.
2. Add all ingredients to a large bowl and mix.
3. Lightly oil a large pie pan.
4. Scoop mixture into pan and cook 45min or until top is golden brown.
5. Divide frittata into 4 servings.

SIDE EACH SERVING WITH:
6oz fruit for a complete lunch

Weight loss Recipes
- no sugar, no flour, made deliciously easy -
WeightLossRecipesCookbook.com

Creamy Tuna Bowl

servings: 4   cooking time: -

INGREDIENTS

- 24oz total: Mixed vegetables (Corn, carrots, peas, green beans)
- 2oz Mayo
- 8oz Cottage cheese
- 8oz Tuna
- 1Tbsp Dijon Mustard
- 2tsp Ranch seasoning (Find seasoning in "Sauces, Seasonings, and Sides")
- Pinch of Sea salt

DIRECTIONS

1. Add all ingredients except vegetables to a large bowl and mix.
2. if vegetables are frozen microwave 3-4min to thaw.
3. Fold in vegetables.
4. Divide mixture into 4 containers.

SIDE EACH SERVING WITH:
6oz fruit for a complete lunch

Weight loss Recipes
- no sugar, no flour, made deliciously easy -
WeightLossRecipesCookbook.com

Cheesecake Lentil Berry Bars

servings: 4 cooking time: 55min

INGREDIENTS

- 12oz Cooked or canned lentils
- 12oz Banana
- 12oz Mixed berries
- 1 Egg
- 2oz Peanut butter
- 1oz Oven roasted peanuts
- 1/2tsp Baking soda
- 2tsp of each: Cinnamon, almond extract
- Pinch of Sea salt
- 4oz Cream cheese

DIRECTIONS

1. Preheat oven to 375.
2. Blend lentils with a hand blender or food processor until smooth.
3. Add banana, egg, baking soda, cinnamon, almond extract, salt, cream cheese, peanut butter, and mix/mash.
4. Lightly oil a medium baking dish.
5. Scoop mixture into dish and sprinkle with berries and another pinch of cinnamon.
6. Bake 45min.
7. Let cool 10min or refrigerate overnight for best texture.
8. Divide into 4 servings.

SIDE EACH SERVING WITH:
6oz vegetables for a complete lunch

Weight loss Recipes
- no sugar, no flour, made deliciously easy -
WeightLossRecipesCookbook.com

Turkey Stuffing Muffies

servings: 4   cooking time: 35min

INGREDIENTS

- 1 12oz Bag frozen cauliflower rice
- 1 12oz Bag frozen peas and carrots
- 8oz Cooked ground turkey
- 4oz Shredded cheese
- 4 Eggs
- 1tsp of each: Thyme, sage, rosemary, onion powder
- 1/2tsp Garlic salt

DIRECTIONS

1. Preheat oven to 375.
2. Heat and lightly oil a skillet.
3. Add ground turkey to skillet and brown.
4. Add cooked ground turkey, eggs, cheese, and spices to a large bowl and mix.
5. Add frozen vegetables and mix.
6. Divide mixture into 2 12muffin, muffin pans.
7. Bake 35min.

6 MUFFINS = 1 SERVING.
SIDE EACH SERVING WITH:
6oz fruit for a complete lunch

Weight loss Recipes
- no sugar, no flour, made deliciously easy -
WeightLossRecipesCookbook.com

Blueberry Goat Cheese Scones

servings: 2   cooking time: 30

INGREDIENTS

- 6oz Canned chickpeas (1/2 protein)
- 8oz Banana (2/3 fruit)
- 4oz Frozen blueberries (1/3 fruit)
- 2tsp of each: Latte spice, vanilla extract (Find Latte spice in "Sauces, Seasonings, and Sides")
- 1/2tsp Baking soda
- Pinch of Sea salt
- 2oz Goat cheese (full fat or ½ protein)

DIRECTIONS

1. Preheat oven to 375.
2. Drain and blend chickpeas with a hand blender or food processor until smooth.
3. Add all ingredients except blueberries and mash/mix.
4. Stir in blueberries.
5. Line a baking pan with parchment paper and scoop mixture onto pan.
6. Bake 30min.

SIDE EACH SERVING WITH:
6oz vegetables, and ½ protein or a fat for a complete lunch

Weight loss Recipes
- no sugar, no flour, made deliciously easy -
WeightLossRecipesCookbook.com

Tuna Casserole Bars

servings: 4   cooking time: 35

INGREDIENTS

- 8oz total: 1 Small can tuna, cottage cheese
- 4 Eggs
- 4oz Shredded cheddar cheese
- 1 12oz Bag frozen peas and carrots
- 1 12oz Bag frozen spinach
- 2tsp Oriental seasoning (Find seasoning in "Sauces, Seasonings, and Sides")
- Pinch of each: Sea salt, baking soda

DIRECTIONS

1. Preheat oven to 375.
2. Mix eggs, tuna, cottage cheese, and seasonings.
3. Add frozen vegetables and mix.
4. Line a pan with parchment paper.
5. Scoop mixture onto pan and bake 15min.
6. Sprinkle with cheese and bake another 20min.
7. Divide pan into 4 servings.

SIDE EACH SERVING WITH:
6oz fruit for a complete lunch.

41

Weight loss Recipes
- no sugar, no flour, made deliciously easy -
WeightLossRecipesCookbook.com

Coconut Berry Bars

servings: 3   cooking time: 40min

INGREDIENTS

- 1 1/2oz Unsweetened coconut flakes
- 3oz Walnuts
- 3 Eggs
- 12oz Banana
- 6oz Frozen mixed berries
- 2tsp Coconut extract
- Pinch of Sea salt

DIRECTIONS

1. Preheat oven to 375.
2. Add all ingredients to a large bowl and mash/mix.
3. Lightly oil a medium baking pan.
4. Scoop mixture into pan
5. Bake 40min.
6. Cut into bars and divide into 3 servings.

SIDE EACH SERVING WITH:
6oz vegetables for a complete lunch.

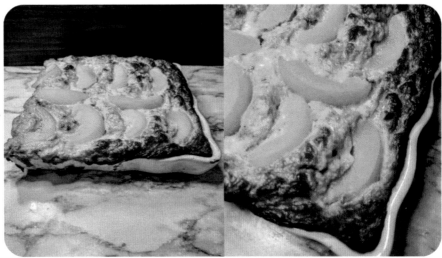

Peach Cheddar Bars

servings: 2   cooking time: 30min

INGREDIENTS

- 2oz Shredded cheddar cheese
- 6oz Canned chickpeas
- 2 Eggs
- 1tsp of each: Cinnamon, vanilla extract
- Pinch of Sea salt
- 1/2tsp of each: Baking soda, baking powder
- 10oz Banana
- 4oz Peaches

DIRECTIONS

1. Preheat oven to 375.
2. Lightly oil a medium baking dish.
3. Drain and blend chickpeas with a hand blender or food processor until smooth.
4. Add all ingredients to chickpeas except peaches and mash/mix.
5. Pour mixture into baking dish and top with peaches.
6. Bake 30min.
7. Divide into 2 servings.

SIDE EACH SERVING WITH:
6oz vegetables for a complete lunch.

Weight loss Recipes
- no sugar, no flour, made deliciously easy -
WeightLossRecipesCookbook.com

Blueberry Chia Bars

servings: 4   cooking time: 30min

INGREDIENTS

- 2oz Chia seeds
- 2oz Peanut butter
- 1lb 2oz Banana
- 6oz Frozen blueberries
- 1/2tsp of each: Baking soda, baking powder, vanilla extract
- Pinch of Sea salt
- 4 Eggs
- 1oz Walnuts

DIRECTIONS

1. Preheat oven to 375.
2. Add all ingredients to a bowl and mash/mix.
3. Bake 30min.
4. Divide into 4 servings

SIDE EACH SERVING WITH:
6oz vegetables for a complete lunch.

Weight loss Recipes
- no sugar, no flour, made deliciously easy -
WeightLossRecipesCookbook.com

Gingerbread Pecan Blondies

servings: 3   cooking time: 30min

INGREDIENTS

- 9oz Canned chickpeas
- 2Tbsp Gingerbread spice (Find seasoning in "Sauces, Seasonings, and Sides")
- 1Tbsp + 1tsp Maple extract
- 1 1/2oz Peanut butter
- 1oz Goat cheese (or you can do 3oz total of pecans)
- 2oz Pecans
- 18oz Banana
- 1tsp of each: Baking soda, cinnamon
- 1/2tsp Sea salt

SIDE EACH SERVING WITH:
6oz vegetables for a complete lunch.

DIRECTIONS

1. Preheat oven to 375.
2. Drain and blend chickpeas with a hand blender or food processor until smooth.
3. Add 12oz banana, 1Tbsp maple extract, gingerbread spice, salt, peanut butter, baking soda, and mash/mix.
4. Line a baking pan with parchment paper and spread mixture 1/2in thick on pan.
5. Using the same bowl mash 6oz banana.
6. Add pecans, 1tsp maple extract, a pinch of salt, goat cheese, and cinnamon.
7. Dollop pecan mixture on top of chickpea mixture and gently spread.
8. Bake 30min.
9. Let cool before dividing into 3 servings.

Weight loss Recipes
- no sugar, no flour, made deliciously easy -
WeightLossRecipesCookbook.com

Green Bean Quiche

servings: 4   cooking time: 30min

INGREDIENTS

- 24oz Frozen green beans
- 4 Eggs
- 8oz Cottage cheese
- 4oz Shredded cheese
- 1tsp Sea salt
- 2Tbsp Greek seasoning (Find seasoning in "Sauces, Seasonings, and Sides")

DIRECTIONS

1. Preheat oven to 375.
2. Add all ingredients except green beans to a large bowl and mix.
3. Fold in frozen green beans.
4. Lightly oil a 9x13 cake pan.
5. Pour mixture into pan and bake 40-45min or until the edges are starting to brown.
6. Let cool 5min before dividing into 4 servings.

SIDE EACH SERVING WITH:
6oz vegetables for a complete lunch or side each serving with 8oz vegetables for a complete dinner

Weight loss Recipes
- no sugar, no flour, made deliciously easy -
WeightLossRecipesCookbook.com

Asian Scrabble Stir Fry

servings: 4   cooking time: 10min

INGREDIENTS

- 4 Eggs
- 1Tbsp Soy sauce
- 1/2oz Toasted sesame oil
- 3oz Shredded cheese
- 24oz Frozen Sugar snap pea stir fry mix
- Pinch of Everything But The Bagel Seasoning

DIRECTIONS

1. Heat and lightly oil a large skillet.
2. Add frozen vegetables and sauté 6-7min.
3. Whisk eggs, soy sauce, sesame oil, and cheese.
4. Pour egg mixture into skillet and stir until eggs are scrambled.
5. Divide into 4 servings and sprinkle with Everything But The Bagel Seasoning.

SIDE EACH SERVING WITH:
6oz fruit for a complete lunch

Weight loss Recipes
- no sugar, no flour, made deliciously easy -
WeightLossRecipesCookbook.com

Pumpkin Nut Cheesecake Bars

servings: 5   cooking time: 60min

INGREDIENTS

- 15oz Canned chickpeas
- 15oz Canned pumpkin
- 15oz Banana
- 5oz Cream cheese
- 2 1/2oz Peanut butter
- 2 1/2oz total: Ground flax seed, peanuts, walnuts, pecans, almonds
- 1tsp Baking soda
- Pinch of each: Sea salt, instant coffee
- 2Tbsp Pumpkin pie spice (Find seasoning in "Sauces, Seasonings, and Sides")
- 1Tbsp Maple extract
- 2tsp Cinnamon

SIDE EACH SERVING WITH:
6oz vegetables for a complete lunch

DIRECTIONS

1. Preheat oven to 375.
2. Drain and blend chickpeas with a hand blender or food processor until smooth.
3. Add banana to chickpeas and mash.
4. Add cream cheese, peanut butter, nuts, baking soda, sea salt, pumpkin pie spice, maple extract, pumpkin, and mash/mix.
5. Line a baking pan with parchment paper.
6. Scoop mixture onto lined pan and spread 1/2in thick.
7. Sprinkle with salt, cinnamon, and instant coffee.
8. Bake 45min.
9. Let cool 10-20min before cutting into 5 servings.

Weight loss Recipes
- no sugar, no flour, made deliciously easy -
WeightLossRecipesCookbook.com

Spinach Tuna Melt

servings: 4   cooking time: 50min

INGREDIENTS

- 4oz Canned tuna
- 4oz Shredded cheddar cheese
- 6 Eggs
- 1Tbsp Dijon mustard
- 1/2tsp of each: Turmeric, ginger, sea salt
- 1tsp Paprika
- 25oz total frozen: Onions peppers, spinach

DIRECTIONS

1. Preheat oven to 375.
2. Add all ingredients to a large bowl except vegetables and mix.
3. Stir in vegetables.
4. Lightly oil a med/large baking dish.
5. Pour mixture into baking dish and bake 45-50min.
6. Cut into 4 bars.

SIDE EACH SERVING WITH:
6oz fruit for a complete lunch or side each serving with 8oz vegetables for a complete dinner

Weight loss Recipes
- no sugar, no flour, made deliciously easy -
WeightLossRecipesCookbook.com

Blueberry Blondie Muffies

servings: 3   cooking time: 30min

INGREDIENTS

- 3 Eggs
- 3oz Canned chickpeas
- 1/2oz Ground flax seed
- 1/2oz Walnuts (or your favorite nuts)
- 2oz Peanut butter (or your favorite nut butter)
- 2oz Whole milk ricotta cheese
- 6oz Frozen blueberries
- 12oz Banana

DIRECTIONS

1. Preheat oven to 375.
2. Drain and blend chickpeas with a hand blender or food processor until smooth.
3. Mash banana.
4. Add all ingredients to a large bowl and mix.
5. Lightly oil or line a muffin pan (I used a deep heart muffin pan).
6. Divide mixture into muffin pan and bake 30min.
7. Divide muffins into 3 servings.

SIDE EACH SERVING WITH:
6oz vegetables for a complete lunch

Weight loss Recipes
- no sugar, no flour, made deliciously easy -
WeightLossRecipesCookbook.com

50

Ricotta Gnocchi

servings: 2 cooking time: 30min

INGREDIENTS

- 5oz Ricotta cheese (shrinks to 4oz) (full fat)
- 1 Egg (1/4 protein)
- 1oz Ground flax seed (1/4 protein)
- 4oz Spaghetti sauce (condiment)
- 1tsp of each: Basil, chives
- Pinch of each: Sea salt, pepper

DIRECTIONS

1. Preheat oven to 375.
2. Line a plate with a towel or 2-3 layers of paper towels.
3. Spread ricotta onto towel, fold towel over ricotta and gently press.
4. Let sit 15min to release excess water.
5. Mix ricotta, egg, seasonings, and flax seed.
6. Lightly oil a baking pan.
7. Using your hands roll/divide ricotta mixture into 18 balls and place on baking pan.
8. Bake 10-15min or until the edges are slightly golden brown.
9. Pour spaghetti sauce into a skillet or pot and heat/simmer.
10. Divide sauce into 2 bowls and top with ½ of baked Gnocchi.

SIDE EACH SERVING WITH:
½ protein, 6oz vegetables, and 6oz fruit for a complete lunch. Or side with 14oz vegetables and ½ protein for a complete dinner.

Weight loss Recipes
- no sugar, no flour, made deliciously easy -
WeightLossRecipesCookbook.com

Spinach Apple Fritters

servings: 3   cooking time: 10min

INGREDIENTS

- 6 Eggs
- 3oz Shredded cheese
- 18oz Apple
- 1/2tsp Baking soda
- Pinch of Sea salt
- 20oz Frozen spinach

DIRECTIONS

1. Heat and lightly oil a pancake maker, a griddle, or a skillet.
2. Dice apple.
3. Add all ingredients to a large bowl and mix.
4. Scoop mixture into maker and cook 7-10min or pour mixture onto griddle or skillet and cook 5-6min each side.
5. Divide fritters into 3 servings.

Weight loss Recipes
- no sugar, no flour, made deliciously easy -
WeightLossRecipesCookbook.com

Fruity Chia Bars

servings: 3 cooking time: 30min

INGREDIENTS

- 3 Eggs
- 1 1/2oz Chia seeds
- 6oz Cottage cheese
- 12oz Banana
- 12oz total frozen: Mango, blueberries
- 1/2tsp of each: Sea salt, baking soda, baking powder
- 1tsp Vanilla extract

DIRECTIONS

1. Preheat oven to 350.
2. Line a baking pan with parchment paper.
3. Mash banana.
4. Add all ingredients to banana and mash.
5. Pour mixture onto baking pan.
6. Bake 30min.
7. Cut into bars and divide into 3 servings.

SIDE EACH SERVING WITH:
6oz vegetables for a complete lunch.

Weight loss Recipes
- no sugar, no flour, made deliciously easy -
WeightLossRecipesCookbook.com

Tuna Cakes

servings: 3 cooking time: 45min

INGREDIENTS

- 3 Eggs
- 6oz Canned tuna
- 24oz Deluxe stir fry (sugar snap peas, baby corn, broccoli, bell peppers, water chestnuts)
- 1Tbsp Dijon mustard
- 3oz Shredded cheese
- Pinch of Sea salt

DIRECTIONS

1. Preheat oven to 375.
2. Add all ingredients to a bowl except vegetables and mix.
3. Add vegetables and mix.
4. Line or lightly oil a baking pan.
5. Using your hands, grab a handful of mixture and press into a patty and place on pan.
6. Repeat with remaining mixture.
7. Bake 45min or until top is starting to brown.
8. Divide patties into 3 servings

SIDE EACH SERVING WITH:
6oz fruit for a complete lunch.

Dinner

1 PROTEIN, 1 FAT, 14OZ VEGETABLES

Shock Your Brain

When I started meal prepping for my Uncle Tim, it was OVERWHELMING! Let me give you a little back story. When my Uncle Tim (my dad's younger brother) was a toddler, he was diagnosed with Prader-Willi. Some of the symptoms of Prader-Willi are small feet and hands, constant hunger, and in extreme cases, they can eat until they die. Thankfully Tim's case is not this extreme but he does have to be watched and he lives in a group home. My dad is his legal guardian.

TIM'S 54TH BIRTHDAY

Fast forward to February 2021. Tim had started experiencing some health problems with breathing and fainting spells. One night, he was at our kid's program at church where he had fainted and broke his arm. That's when his health really started to plummet. He went into a nursing home to recover and it became his prison! With covid, there was limited interaction with others (which is very hard for Tim as he is a social guy.) He became depressed. We tried and tried to get him back into the group home he lived in and 3 months later we finally got him out! He was still experiencing breathing problems and was having a hard time adjusting to being back at home. It seemed like every weekend dad would get a call that Tim went into the emergency room. The expected life span for people diagnosed with Prader-Willi is

50 years old. Tim is 55. The Doctors were telling us to expect the worst and to say our last goodbyes.

One morning during my time with God, this thought came to me. *"What would happen if Tim cut out sugar, flour, and lost weight?"* I know the health benefits I have experienced have been amazing! I didn't know how this would work because Tim lives in a home and they provide all of his meals. So, I brought it up to mom and dad. I offered to meal prep all of Tim's meals and we could bring them to his home. They were excited about it. My dad called Tim's home and they agreed!

When God has a plan, He makes all the pieces fit together. We don't have to struggle to make it happen. We just follow Him.

St. Patricks day 2022

I started meal prepping for Tim and week one was exciting. Week two was cool. Week 3 was work. Then, we were going to go on vacation so that meant I had to meal prep for two weeks! That was...oof! It was overwhelming. I thought, *"How can I keep this up? My schedule is busy without this meal prepping...and is this even making a difference?"*

Tim did go to the emergency room a couple more times. What was amazing was, his home asked the hospital if they could bring the meals I had made for him to eat to the hospital, and THE HOSPITAL AGREED!! I was shocked!

We finally got Tim's breathing problem figured out, and we were starting to see some progress with his health. His eyes were clearer, he was more alert, his walking had improved, and he was starting to have actual conversations. I was figuring out a good pace with the meal prepping and I started to create batch meals in larger quantities that really helped with the mental part of meal prepping. Tim started to lose weight and his clothes started to get baggier and baggier!

There is a very skilled guitar teacher who is fascinated with the learning process. He had a piece of music he wanted to play but it was a very hard piece to play. Everyone who tried to play this song would take the entire song and try to learn it all at once. However, this guy had a different approach. He took only four notes from one part of the song, put a mindless show on tv, sat on his couch, and played the four notes over, and over, and over, and over, for almost 10 hours. He said when he did this it shocked his brain into thinking, *"I have to get better,"* and he did. He said this part of the song started to feel slower and easier to play. He continued to do this until he mastered the whole song.

We did that SAME exact thing when we made the change to our complete diet and way of eating. At first, it felt overwhelming, but as we kept with it, something clicked. Our brain was shocked into getting better until it became second

So we're not giving up. How could we! Even though on the outside it often looks like things are falling apart on us, on the inside, where God is making new life, not a day goes by without his unfolding grace. These hard times are small potatoes compared to the coming good times, the lavish celebration prepared for us. There's far more here than meets the eye. The things we see now are here today, gone tomorrow. But the things we can't see now will last forever.
2 Corinthinas 4:16-18
MSG

nature. It became slower. It takes less mental energy now.

It was the same with meal prepping for Tim. Now, I can make his full week of meals within 2-3hrs in one day. That includes dividing, labeling, packaging, and putting all the ingredients away.

When life feels overwhelming, it doesn't mean you should quit. It means we need to simplify and work on one thing at a time until that is mastered. You can make yourself get used to anything. Stick with it. It will get easier and easier every day!

With shocking joy,
Natalie and Tim

2 Corinthians 4:16-18 AMPC *"Therefore we do not become discouraged (utterly spiritless, exhausted, and wearied out through fear). Though our outer man is [progressively] decaying and wasting away, yet our inner self is being [progressively] renewed day after day.*
17 For our light, momentary affliction (this slight distress of the passing hour) is ever more and more abundantly preparing and producing and achieving for us an everlasting weight of glory [beyond all measure, excessively surpassing all comparisons and all calculations, a vast and transcendent glory and blessedness never to cease!],
18 Since we consider and look not to the things that are seen but to the things that are unseen; for the things that are visible are temporal (brief and fleeting), but the things that are invisible are deathless and everlasting.

Weight loss Recipes
- no sugar, no flour, made deliciously easy -
WeightLossRecipesCookbook.com

Asian Stir Fry
Batch Cook

servings: 3-5   cooking time: 25 min

INGREDIENTS

- 1oz of each: Soy sauce, apple cider vinegar
- 1tsp of each: Onion powder, garlic powder
- 1/2tsp Turmeric
- 2tsp of each: Ginger, minced garlic
- 2 12oz bags Frozen broccoli
- 2 10oz bags Frozen zucchini
- 1 12oz Bag of each: frozen kale or spinach, carrots, cauliflower

DIRECTIONS

1. Heat and lightly oil a large pot or wok.
2. Add vegetables to pot and cook 20min or until tender stirring occasionally.
3. In a separate bowl add remaining ingredients and mix.
4. Pour sauce mixture into pot and mix.
5. Cook another 1-2min.
6. Divide vegetable mixture into 14oz servings for dinner or 6oz servings for lunch.

SIDE EACH SERVING WITH:
a protein and fat for a complete dinner

Weight loss Recipes
- no sugar, no flour, made deliciously easy -
WeightLossRecipesCookbook.com

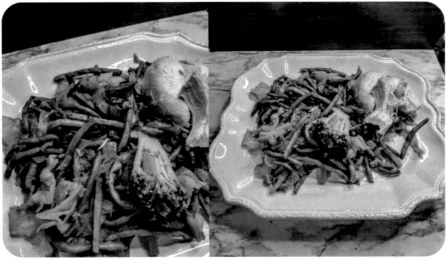

Oriental Stir Fry Bowl

servings: 5-6   cooking time: 2hr

INGREDIENTS

- 1 Whole chicken
- ½ Head of cabbage
- 1 Large bag Frozen Asian stir fry vegetables
- 2 12oz bag Frozen long string beans
- 3 Med Onion
- 1 Tbsp of each: Soy sauce, apple cider vinegar
- 2-3Tbsp Oriental Seasoning
- Pinch of Sea salt
- 3-4 Cloves garlic

DIRECTIONS

1. Preheat oven to 350 and bake chicken for 2hrs or until internal temp is at least 165.
2. Heat and lightly oil a large pot or wok.
3. Dice onion, garlic, and cabbage.
4. Add onion to pot and sauté 3-4min.
5. Add cabbage and frozen vegetables to pot.
6. Sprinkle with seasonings.
7. Cover and stir occasionally 15-20min or until vegetables are tender.
8. Add 14oz of vegetables to a large bowl or plate.
9. Top with 4oz cooked chicken and side with a fat.

Weight loss Recipes
- no sugar, no flour, made deliciously easy -
WeightLossRecipesCookbook.com

Green Bean Soup

servings: 5-6   cooking time: 25 min

INGREDIENTS

- 2 10oz Bag frozen chopped onion
- 5 12oz Bag frozen green beans
- 2 12oz Bag Frozen chopped spinach
- 1Tbsp of each: Onion powder, garlic powder, basil, parsley
- Pinch of each: Sea salt, rosemary, thyme
- 2lb Vegetable broth

DIRECTIONS

1. Heat and lightly oil a large pot.
2. Add onion and sauté 3-4min.
3. Add remaining ingredients, mix, and bring to a boil.
4. Reduce heat to med and simmer 15min or until vegetables are tender.
5. Strain vegetables into 14oz portions.
6. Divide remaining broth in the pot into each container of vegetables.

SIDE EACH SERVING WITH:

a protein and fat to each portion. I did 6oz beans, 1oz cheese
or 3oz beans, 2oz ricotta cheese, and 1oz cheese
or 2oz tuna, 2oz ricotta, and 1oz cheese.

Weight loss Recipes
- no sugar, no flour, made deliciously easy -
WeightLossRecipesCookbook.com

Bacon Vegetable Lasagna

servings: 2   cooking time: 1hr

INGREDIENTS

- 1oz Cooked turkey bacon
- 4oz Ricotta cheese
- 1 Egg
- 2 1/2oz Shredded cheese
- 3/4tsp of each: Onion powder, garlic powder, parsley, basil, lemon juice
- Pinch of Garlic salt
- 4oz Spaghetti sauce
- 30oz total frozen: Zucchini, broccoli, asparagus, cauliflower, green beans, carrots

DIVIDE CASSEROLE INTO 2 SERVINGS

DIRECTIONS

1. Preheat oven to 350.
2. Pour a little spaghetti sauce into the bottom of a large baking dish.
3. Tilt to evenly distribute sauce.
4. Add half of vegetables to baking dish and top with 2oz spaghetti sauce.
5. In a separate bowl add ricotta, egg, seasonings, lemon juice, and mix.
6. Scoop ½ of ricotta mixture onto vegetables.
7. Top with half of cheese.
8. Add remaining vegetables, spaghetti sauce, ricotta mixture, and cheese.
9. Crumble bacon and sprinkle on top.
10. Bake 1hr or until vegetables are tender.

Weight loss Recipes
- no sugar, no flour, made deliciously easy -
WeightLossRecipesCookbook.com

Lasagna Bowl

servings: 4-6   cooking time: 25 min

INGREDIENTS

- 1Lb Ground beef
- 1 15oz Container ricotta cheese
- 2 10oz Bag of each: Frozen cauliflower, frozen kale, frozen zucchini, frozen chopped onions
- 1 12oz Bag frozen broccoli and cauliflower
- 1Tbsp of each: Onion powder, garlic powder
- 2Tbsp of each: Oregano, parsley, basil
- 1 24oz Jar spaghetti sauce
- 1 14.5oz Can Fire roasted tomatoes

DIRECTIONS

1. Brown/cook beef.
2. Heat and lightly oil a large pot.
3. Add onion and sauté 2-3min.
4. Add remaining frozen vegetables and seasonings to pot and cook 20min or until vegetables are tender.

SIDE EACH SERVING WITH:
Divide 4oz Cooked beef, 2oz spaghetti sauce, and 2oz ricotta cheese into each container. Add 14oz cooked vegetables to each container and mix.

Creamy Vegetables Chowder

servings: 6   cooking time: 45 min

INGREDIENTS

- 12oz Whole milk ricotta cheese
- 9oz Canned chickpeas
- 1Tbsp of each: Garlic powder, onion powder, minced garlic
- 1Tbsp of each: Parsley, basil
- 1tsp Thyme
- 3Lbs Vegetable broth
- 5lbs 8oz total: 3 Onions, frozen cauliflower, frozen broccoli, frozen carrots, frozen green beans, frozen peas and carrots (weigh onion after cooking)

DIRECTIONS

1. Heat and lightly oil a large pot.
2. Dice onions.
3. Add onions to pot and sauté 3-4min or until golden.
4. Remove onions from pot to weigh.
5. Add onions, broth, and cauliflower to pot and bring to a boil.
6. Reduce heat and simmer 15min or until cauliflower is tender.
7. Use an immersion blender or work in batches with a blender and blend soup.
8. Add remaining vegetables to blended soup and simmer 25-30min or until tender.
9. Drain and blend chickpeas with a hand blender or food processor until smooth.
10. Add ricotta, seasonings, and chickpeas to soup and simmer 5-10min longer.
11. Divide soup into 6 containers.

SIDE EACH SERVING WITH:
¾ protein for a complete dinner.

Weight loss Recipes
- no sugar, no flour, made deliciously easy -
WeightLossRecipesCookbook.com

Squash Chili

servings: 4   cooking time: 50 min

INGREDIENTS

- 2Lbs Vegetable broth
- 8oz Cooked ground beef
- 12oz total: Cannellini beans, black beans
- 4oz Shredded cheese
- 30oz total frozen: Butternut squash, carrots, broccoli, cauliflower, green beans
- 2tsp of each: Sage, cumin
- 1tsp of each: Chili powder, thyme, rosemary, basil
- Pinch of Sea salt
- 4Tbsp Tomato paste

DIRECTIONS

1. Add all ingredients except cheese to a large pot and bring to a boil.
2. Reduce heat and simmer 45min.
3. Divide chili into 4 containers and top each container with 1oz cheese.

Weight loss Recipes
- no sugar, no flour, made deliciously easy -
WeightLossRecipesCookbook.com

Pizza Lasagna

servings: 2   cooking time: 1hr

INGREDIENTS

- 30oz total: Cooked spaghetti squash, frozen broccoli, onion, frozen carrots, frozen green beans, frozen asparagus or your favorite vegetables
- 1 Egg
- 4oz Cottage cheese
- 1oz Turkey pepperoni
- 1 1/2oz Shredded cheese
- 2oz Whole milk ricotta cheese
- 1Tbsp of each: Parsley, basil
- 1/2Tbsp of each: Onion powder, garlic powder
- Pinch of Garlic salt
- 4oz Spaghetti sauce

DIRECTIONS

1. Preheat oven to 375.
2. Pour 2oz spaghetti sauce into the bottom of a medium/large baking dish.
3. Add vegetables to baking dish.
4. Cut pepperonis into 4ths.
5. In a separate bowl mix remaining ingredients.
6. Pour mixture on top of vegetables and bake 1hr

DIVIDE CASSEROLE INTO 2 SERVINGS

Weight loss Recipes
- no sugar, no flour, made deliciously easy -
WeightLossRecipesCookbook.com

Enchilada Casserole

servings: 3   cooking time: 1hr

INGREDIENTS

- 2lbs 8oz total frozen: Cauliflower rice, peppers, onions, carrots, broccoli, or your favorite vegetables
- 9oz Cooked taco beef
- 3oz Shredded cheese
- Enchilada sauce (find sauce recipe in "Sauces, Seasonings, and Sides")
- 6oz Can fire roasted tomatoes

DIRECTIONS

1. Preheat oven to 375.
2. Add vegetables to a large casserole dish.
3. Top with fire roasted tomatoes, taco beef, and drizzle with enchilada sauce.
4. Sprinkle with cheese and cover.
5. Bake 1hr or until vegetables are tender.

DIVIDE CASSEROLE INTO 3 SERVINGS

Weight loss Recipes
- no sugar, no flour, made deliciously easy -
WeightLossRecipesCookbook.com

Butter Nut Squash Casserole

servings: 3   cooking time: 2hr

INGREDIENTS

- 3lbs total frozen: Butter nut squash, peas, carrots, asparagus, cauliflower
- 6oz Canned crushed tomatoes
- 3oz Shredded cheddar cheese
- 6oz Ricotta cheese
- 4oz Yogurt
- 2 Eggs
- 3Tbsp Lemon juice
- 1Tbsp of each: Garlic powder, onion powder, minced garlic, nutritional yeast, parsley, basil
- 1tsp Rosemary
- Pinch of each: Garlic salt, thyme, sage

DIRECTIONS

1. Preheat oven to 375.
2. Spread some of the canned tomatoes onto the bottom of a large baking dish.
3. Add frozen vegetables to dish.
4. Pour remaining tomatoes on top of vegetables.
5. In a separate bowl mix remaining ingredients and pour on top.
6. Cover and bake 2hrs or until vegetables are tender.

DIVIDE CASSEROLE INTO 3 SERVINGS

Weight loss Recipes
- no sugar, no flour, made deliciously easy -
WeightLossRecipesCookbook.com

69

Oriental Casserole

servings: 3   cooking time: 2hr

INGREDIENTS

- 3lbs total: Frozen cauliflower, frozen carrots, frozen asparagus, frozen peas, frozen carrots, onion
- 6oz Canned crushed tomatoes
- 2Tbsp of each: Apple cider vinegar, minced garlic, oriental seasoning (find seasoning recipe in "Sauces, Seasonings, and Sides")
- 1tsp Curry powder
- Pinch of each: Garlic salt, turmeric, Everything But The Bagel Seasoning
- 6oz Ricotta cheese
- 2 Eggs
- 3oz Shredded cheddar cheese
- 1Tbsp of each: Nutritional yeast, parsley

DIRECTIONS

1. Preheat oven to 375.
2. Spread some of the canned tomatoes onto the bottom of a large baking dish.
3. Add frozen vegetables to dish.
4. Dice onion and add to baking dish.
5. Pour remaining tomatoes onto vegetables.
6. In a separate bowl mix remaining ingredients except Everything But The Bagel Seasoning.
7. Pour mixture on top of vegetables and sprinkle with Everything But The Bagel Seasoning.
8. Cover and bake 2hrs or until vegetables are tender.

DIVIDE CASSEROLE INTO 3 SERVINGS

Weight loss Recipes
- no sugar, no flour, made deliciously easy -
WeightLossRecipesCookbook.com

Mushroom Squash Swiss

servings: 3   cooking time: 30min

INGREDIENTS

- 3lbs total: White sliced mushrooms, onion, frozen broccoli, 3 Roma tomatoes, 1 small Hubbard squash
- 1Tbsp of each: Minced garlic, basil
- 3Tbsp Nutritional yeast
- 6oz Ricotta cheese
- 6oz Plain Greek yogurt
- 9oz Cooked steak
- 1tsp of each: Rosemary, sea salt
- 3/4tsp of each: Garlic powder, onion powder
- 10oz Chicken or vegetable broth

DIVIDE CASSEROLE INTO 3 SERVINGS AND TOP EACH SERVING WITH 3OZ COOKED STEAK

DIRECTIONS

1. Heat and lightly oil a large saucepan.
2. Slice onion and tomatoes.
3. Peel, core, and dice squash.
4. Wash mushrooms.
5. Add onions to pan and sauté 2-3min or until starting to brown.
6. Add mushrooms, tomatoes, salt, squash and sauté 2-3min.
7. Add broccoli, minced garlic, onion powder, garlic powder, and 1Tbsp nutritional yeast.
8. Cook 2min longer.
9. In a separate bowl mix 2Tbsp nutritional yeast, ricotta, broth, and yogurt.
10. Add yogurt mixture to pan and mix.
11. Reduce heat to low and simmer 15-20min or until vegetables are tender.

Weight loss Recipes
- no sugar, no flour, made deliciously easy -
WeightLossRecipesCookbook.com

Turkey Dinner Soup

servings: 7   cooking time: 43min

INGREDIENTS

- 2 12oz Bags frozen cauliflower rice
- 1 12oz Bag of each: frozen spinach, frozen peas and carrots, frozen green beans
- 1 10oz Bag Seasoning blend (peppers, onions)
- 1 3lb Carton chicken or vegetable broth
- 1Tbsp of each: Garlic powder, thyme
- 2tsp of each: Sage, rosemary
- 1tsp Garlic salt
- 2oz Cooked ground turkey
- 3oz Canned black beans
- 1oz Shredded cheese

DIRECTIONS

1. Heat and lightly oil a large pot.
2. Add seasoning blend and sauté 2-3min.
3. Add remaining vegetables, broth, and sprinkle with seasonings.
4. Bring to a boil.
5. Reduce heat and simmer 30-40min
6. Strain 14oz of vegetables into each container.
7. Divide remaining broth into each container.
8. Add 2oz ground turkey, 3oz black beans, and 1oz of cheese to each container for a complete dinner.

Weight loss Recipes
- no sugar, no flour, made deliciously easy -
WeightLossRecipesCookbook.com

Cheeseburger Pizza Bowl

servings: 7   cooking time: 30min

INGREDIENTS

- 1 12oz Bag frozen spinach
- 5 12oz Bags frozen California mix (broccoli, carrots, cauliflower)
- 1 10oz Bag frozen seasoning mix (onions, peppers)
- 1 28oz Can crushed tomatoes
- 14oz Sliced black olives
- 14oz Cooked ground beef
- 7oz Shredded cheese
- 3Tbsp Pizza Seasoning (find seasoning recipe in "Sauces, Seasonings, and Sides")
- 1Tbsp Minced garlic

DIRECTIONS

1. Add all vegetables, and crushed tomatoes to a large pot.
2. Heat over high heat 2-3min.
3. Reduce heat from pot to med/high.
4. Add pizza seasoning and olives.
5. Heat a separate skillet and brown beef.
6. Cook 20-30min or until vegetables are tender.

ADD 2OZ BEEF AND 1OZ CHEESE TO 7 MEAL PREP CONTAINERS. DIVIDE VEGETABLES INTO EACH CONTAINER AND MIX

Weight loss Recipes
- no sugar, no flour, made deliciously easy -
WeightLossRecipesCookbook.com

Thanksgiving Leftover Casserole

servings: 3   cooking time: 1hr 40min

INGREDIENTS

- 3lbs total frozen or cooked: Peas, carrots, corn, green beans, asparagus, raw onion
- 6oz Cooked turkey
- 2 Eggs
- 4oz Plain Greek yogurt
- 3oz Shredded cheddar cheese
- 1tsp of each: Thyme, rosemary
- 1/2tsp of each: Garlic salt, sage
- 1/2Tbsp of each: Garlic powder, onion powder, nutritional yeast

DIRECTIONS

1. Preheat oven to 375.
2. Lightly oil a large baking dish.
3. Dice onion.
4. Shred turkey and add to baking dish.
5. Top with vegetables.
6. Add onion on top.
7. In a separate bowl whisk egg, yogurt, cheese, and seasonings.
8. Pour mixture on top and cover.
9. Bake 1hr 40min.

DIVIDE CASSEROLE INTO 3 SERVINGS

74

Weight loss Recipes
- no sugar, no flour, made deliciously easy -
WeightLossRecipesCookbook.com

Thankful Turkey Chowder

servings: 3   cooking time: 44min

INGREDIENTS

- 8oz Cooked turkey
- 1oz Shredded mozzarella cheese
- 4oz Plain Greek yogurt
- 1lb 8oz Chicken or vegetable broth
- 1Tbsp of each: Basil, parsley, rosemary, thyme, minced garlic
- 1/2Tbsp of each: Garlic salt, sage, ginger
- 3oz Heavy whipping cream
- 3lbs total: Onion, Frozen green beans, frozen butternut squash, frozen peas, frozen carrots, frozen cauliflower

DIRECTIONS

1. Heat and lightly oil a large pot.
2. Dice onion.
3. Add onion to pot and sauté 1-2min or until golden.
4. Add vegetables, broth, turkey, seasonings, and mix.
5. Bring to a boil.
6. Reduce heat and simmer 30-40min.
7. Add cream and simmer 2min more.
8. Remove from heat.
9. Stir in yogurt and cheese.

DIVIDE SOUP INTO 3 SERVINGS

Weight loss Recipes
- no sugar, no flour, made deliciously easy -
WeightLossRecipesCookbook.com

Tomato Soup and Grilled Cheese

servings: 6   cooking time: 20min

INGREDIENTS

- 6lbs total: 4 Stalks celery, 2 sweet onion, canned tomatoes
- 3lbs Chicken or vegetable broth
- 2Tbsp of each: Garlic powder, onion powder, parsley, basil, minced garlic
- 3/4tsp Onion powder
- 2tsp Garlic salt
- 2oz Egg waffle per serving (2 eggs came out to 2oz cooked)
- 2oz Swiss cheese per serving
- Pinch of each: garlic salt, Everything But The Bagel Seasoning

DIVIDE SOUP INTO 6 SERVINGS AND SIDE EACH SERVING WITH EGG WAFFLE GRILLED CHEESE.

DIRECTIONS

1. Heat and lightly oil a large pot.
2. Dice celery and onion.
3. Add onion and celery to pot and sauté until golden.
4. Add minced garlic and sauté 2min longer.
5. Add celery and tomatoes.
6. Add broth, and seasonings (except onion powder and Everything But The Bagel Seasoning) to pot and bring to a boil.
7. Reduce heat and simmer 12-15min.
8. Heat and lightly oil a waffle maker.
9. Add onion powder, pinch of garlic salt, and 2 eggs to a glass and whisk.
10. Pour 1/2 of egg mixture into waffle maker and sprinkle with Everything But The Bagel Seasoning.
11. Cook 7-10min or until crispy.
12. Repeat with remaining egg mixture.
13. Top half of egg waffles with cheese and top with empty egg waffles.

Weight loss Recipes
- no sugar, no flour, made deliciously easy -
WeightLossRecipesCookbook.com

Cheesy Turkey Casserole

servings: 3   cooking time: 1hr 30min

INGREDIENTS

- 3lbs total frozen: Peas, carrots, zucchini, green beans, corn
- 6oz Cooked turkey
- 4oz Ricotta cheese
- 1 Egg
- 3oz Shredded mozzarella cheese
- 1tsp of each: Sage, rosemary
- 1/2tsp Garlic salt
- 1Tbsp of each: Nutritional yeast, onion powder, garlic powder, parsley, minced garlic

DIRECTIONS

1. Preheat oven to 375.
2. Lightly oil a large casserole dish.
3. Shred turkey.
4. Add vegetables to dish and top with turkey.
5. In a separate bowl mix ricotta, egg, shredded cheese, and seasonings.
6. Spread mixture on top of casserole.
7. Cover and bake 1hr 30min or until top is golden.

DIVIDE CASSEROLE INTO 3 SERVINGS

Weight loss Recipes
- no sugar, no flour, made deliciously easy -
WeightLossRecipesCookbook.com

Vegetable Beef Soup

servings: 6   cooking time: 1hr

INGREDIENTS

- 3lbs Chicken or vegetable broth
- 6lbs total: 1 4oz Can mushrooms, frozen zucchini, frozen asparagus, onion, large can crushed tomatoes, frozen cauliflower
- 12oz Cooked ground beef (about 2lbs raw comes out to 12oz cooked) (weigh after cooking)
- 2Tbsp of each: Minced garlic, garlic powder, onion powder, basil, parsley, nutritional yeast
- 1tsp Rosemary
- 8oz Plain Greek yogurt
- 4oz Shredded mozzarella cheese
- 6oz Black olives
- 6oz Green olives

DIRECTIONS

1. Heat and lightly oil a large pot.
2. Dice onion and mushrooms.
3. Add onions, mushrooms, and minced garlic to pot and sauté 2-3min.
4. In a separate skillet brown beef.
5. Add remaining vegetables to pot.
6. Add all ingredients except yogurt and cheese to pot and bring to a boil.
7. Reduce heat and simmer 40min-1hr or until vegetables are tender.
8. Remove from heat and stir in yogurt and cheese.

DIVIDE CASSEROLE INTO 6 SERVINGS

Weight loss Recipes
- no sugar, no flour, made deliciously easy -
WeightLossRecipesCookbook.com

Creamy Tuscan
Chicken Noodle Soup

servings: 6   cooking time: 1hr

INGREDIENTS

- 1lb 8oz Cooked chicken
- 3lbs Chicken or vegetable broth
- 2Tbsp of each: Arrow root powder, parsley, basil, garlic powder, onion powder, minced garlic
- 1Tbsp of each: Thyme, rosemary
- 1/2Tbsp of each: Garlic salt, turmeric
- Pinch of Sage
- 4lbs total: Mushrooms, onion, eggplant, yellow pepper, frozen peas and carrots, frozen carrots, frozen cauliflower rice
- 2lbs Palmini spaghetti noodles
- 12oz Canned tomatoes or spaghetti sauce
- 12oz Whole milk ricotta cheese

DIVIDE SOUP INTO 6 SERVINGS

DIRECTIONS

1. Preheat oven to 350.
2. Add chicken and 1inch water to a baking dish.
3. Cover and bake chicken 2hrs or until cooked through and tender.
4. Heat and lightly oil a large pot.
5. Dice mushrooms, onion, yellow pepper, and eggplant into small pieces.
6. Add diced vegetables to pot and sauté 5-7min.
7. Add 1/2cup of broth to a bowl and whisk in arrowroot powder.
8. Add frozen veggies, canned tomatoes, broth, arrowroot mixture, and spices to pot and bring to a boil.
9. Reduce heat and simmer 20-25min or until vegetables are tender.
10. Drain and add palmini noodles and ricotta cheese to pot and mix.
11. Shred chicken and stir into soup

Weight loss Recipes
- no sugar, no flour, made deliciously easy -
WeightLossRecipesCookbook.com

Cheesy Artichoke Palmini Pasta Bowl with Rosemary Balsamic Fried Chicken

servings: -   cooking time: 25min

INGREDIENTS

- 2 14oz Cans of artichoke hearts
- 2 Yellow or sweet onions
- 1 10oz Bag frozen mushrooms
- 5-7 Large carrots
- 3 Pints/containers cherry tomatoes
- 4 Cans palmini linguini
- 4Tbsp Nutritional yeast
- 1/2tsp of each: Turmeric, smoked paprika, garlic salt
- 1Tbsp of each: Onion powder, garlic powder, parsley, basil

ADD 14OZ TOTAL OF PALMINI NOODLES AND CARROT MIXTURE TO A BOWL. TOP WITH 4OZ CHICKEN AND SIDE WITH A FAT FOR A COMPLETE DINNER. (FIND CHICKEN RECIPE IN "SAUCES, SEASONINGS, AND SIDES")

DIRECTIONS

1. Heat and lightly oil a large pot.
2. Dice/slice carrots and onion.
3. Add carrots, onions, mushrooms, cherry tomatoes, parsley, and basil to pot and cook on high 15-20min stirring occasionally until carrots are tender.
4. In a separate bowl add remaining seasonings and mix.
5. Reduce heat to low and add seasonings.
6. Using an immersion blender or potato masher, blend vegetables until almost smooth (its ok to leave some chunks for texture).
7. Drain artichoke hearts and palmini noodles.
8. Add some water to a separate pot and bring to a boil.
9. Add palmini noodles to pot.
10. Reduce heat to med/low and cook 3-4min.
11. Add artichoke hearts to carrot mixture and stir.

Weight loss Recipes
- no sugar, no flour, made deliciously easy -
WeightLossRecipesCookbook.com

Turkey Burger Bowl

servings: 7   cooking time: 25min

INGREDIENTS

- 7oz Shredded cheddar cheese
- 1Tbsp of each: Paprika, Dijon mustard + more for topping
- Pinch of Garlic salt
- 7lbs total frozen: Onions peppers, zucchini, green beans, spinach, carrots
- 3lbs Ground turkey

DIRECTIONS

1. Heat and lightly oil a skillet and a large pot.
2. Form ground turkey into 14 patties.
3. Fry turkey patties in skillet 3-5min each side.
4. Add frozen veggies, paprika, and 1Tbsp Dijon mustard to the large pot and cook 15-20min stirring occasionally until vegetables are tender.

DIVIDE VEGETABLES INTO 7 CONTAINERS.
TOP EACH CONTAINER WITH 4OZ
COOKED BURGERS (ABOUT 2 PATTIES
EACH) AND SPRINKLE WITH 1OZ CHEESE.
TOP WITH MORE DIJON MUSTARD.

Weight loss Recipes
- no sugar, no flour, made deliciously easy -
WeightLossRecipesCookbook.com

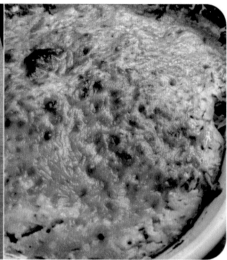

Shepherd's Pie

servings: 2   cooking time: 1hr 20min

INGREDIENTS

- 1 12ozbag Frozen cauliflower
- 19oz total: Peas, carrots, corn, green beans
- 3/4cup Vegetable broth
- 4oz Ground beef (weigh after cooking) (1/2 protein)
- 1oz Ricotta cheese (1/8 protein)
- 2oz Plain Greek yogurt (1/8 protein)
- 3oz Shredded cheese (1/4 protein + full fat)
- 1tsp of each: Onion powder, parsley
- 1/2tsp of each: Rosemary, garlic salt, thyme

DIVIDE CASSEROLE INTO 2 SERVINGS

DIRECTIONS

1. Add broth and cauliflower to a pot.
2. Bring to a boil.
3. Reduce heat and simmer until cauliflower is tender.
4. Using a hand blender or blender, blend cauliflower until smooth.
5. Brown beef.
6. Preheat oven to 375.
7. Lightly oil a medium baking dish.
8. Add mixed vegetables and ground beef to baking dish.
9. In a separate bowl mix ricotta cheese, yogurt, 1oz cheese, cauliflower mixture spices, and mix.
10. Top vegetables with cauliflower mixture and sprinkle with shredded cheese.
11. Cover and bake 45min.
12. Uncover and bake another 10-15min or until edges are starting to brown.

Lasagna Casserole

servings: 2   cooking time: 1hr 5min

INGREDIENTS

- 1lb 4oz or 30oz total frozen: Broccoli, green beans, cauliflower, asparagus, mixed vegetables (vegetables will shrink 1oz when cooked) (full vegetable)
- 1oz Onion
- 4oz Cooked ground beef (1/2 protein)
- 2oz Ricotta cheese (1/2 fat)
- 2oz Kalamata olives (1/2 fat)
- 2oz total: Parmesan cheese, shredded cheese (1/2 protein)
- 4oz Spaghetti sauce (condiment up to 2oz free)
- 1tsp of each: Parsley, basil, oregano, onion powder, garlic powder
- Pinch of Garlic salt

DIRECTIONS

1. Preheat oven to 375.
2. Brown beef.
3. Add all ingredients to a baking dish except parmesan and shredded cheese and mix.
4. Cover and bake 1hr or until vegetables are tender.
5. Uncover and sprinkle with cheese.
6. Bake 5min more to melt cheese.

DIVIDE CASSEROLE INTO 2 SERVINGS

Crispy Pizza Casserole

servings: 2   cooking time: 1hr 25min

INGREDIENTS

- 30oz total: Tomato, coleslaw mix, onion, zucchini, cauliflower, fire roasted tomatoes (vegetables will shrink when cooked) (full vegetable)
- 4oz Spaghetti sauce (condiment)
- 1 Egg (1/4 protein)
- 3oz Canned chickpeas (1/4 protein)
- 2oz Plain Greek yogurt (1/8 protein)
- 1oz Turkey pepperoni (1/8 protein)
- 1oz Shredded cheese (1/4 protein)
- 2tsp of each: Parsley, basil, oregano
- 1tsp Garlic salt
- 3-4 Cloves garlic

DIRECTIONS

1. Preheat oven to 375.
2. Mince garlic, dice tomatoes, and onion.
3. Add vegetables and spaghetti sauce to a medium/large baking dish and mix.
4. Blend chickpeas with a hand blender or food processor until smooth.
5. Cut pepperoni into small pieces.
6. Add remaining ingredients to a bowl and mix.
7. Pour chickpea mixture on top of vegetables
8. Bake 1hr 15min or until veggies are tender and chickpea mixture is golden brown.
9. Let sit 5-10min.

**DIVIDE CASSEROLE INTO 2 SERVINGS
SIDE EACH SERVING WITH A FAT.**

Cheesy Green Bean Casserole

servings: 2   cooking time: 1hr 30min

INGREDIENTS

- 30oz total: Frozen green beans, onion, frozen cauliflower rice (full vegetable)
- 1/3cup Chicken or vegetable broth (condiment)
- 2 Eggs (1/2 protein)
- 6oz Canned chickpeas (1/2 protein)
- 2oz Shredded cheese (full fat)
- 1Tbsp of each: Nutritional yeast, onion powder, Everything But The Bagel Seasoning
- Pinch of each: Curry powder, sea salt

DIRECTIONS

1. Preheat oven to 375 and lightly oil a med/large baking dish.
2. Dice onion.
3. Add frozen vegetables to baking dish and top with onions.
4. Drain and blend chickpeas with a hand blender or food processor until smooth.
5. Add remaining ingredients to blended chickpeas and mix.
6. Top vegetables with chickpea mixture.
7. Bake 1hr 30min or until top is golden brown

DIVIDE CASSEROLE INTO 2 SERVINGS

Weight loss Recipes
- no sugar, no flour, made deliciously easy -
WeightLossRecipesCookbook.com

Cordon Blue Vegetable Lasagna

servings: 3   cooking time: 1hr 30min

INGREDIENTS

- 6oz Ham
- 3lbs total frozen: Zucchini, cauliflower, corn, peas, carrots, green beans, broccoli, onion
- 2oz Shredded cheddar cheese
- 1oz Shredded parmesan cheese
- 6oz Plain Greek yogurt
- 3oz Ricotta cheese
- 1 1/2tsp of each: Garlic powder, onion powder, Dijon mustard
- 3/4tsp of each: Sea salt, paprika, pepper
- 6-8 Cloves garlic

DIRECTIONS

1. Preheat oven to 375.
2. Dice ham and garlic.
3. Lightly oil a baking dish.
4. Add 1lb of vegetables to baking dish and top with 2oz diced ham and 1oz cheddar cheese.
5. Repeat step 4 for 2nd and 3rd layers.
6. In a separate bowl, mix remaining ingredients except parmesan cheese.
7. Scoop cream mixture onto casserole and sprinkle with parmesan cheese.
8. Cover and bake 1hr 30min or until vegetables are tender.

DIVIDE CASSEROLE INTO 3 SERVINGS

Ranch Quichearole

servings: 3   cooking time: 1hr 30min

INGREDIENTS

- 3oz Ham (1/4 protein)
- 2lbs 7oz total: Green pepper, frozen broccoli, frozen zucchini, frozen corn, frozen carrots, onion, frozen peas, frozen green beans, frozen cauliflower (full vegetable)
- 6oz Plain Greek yogurt (1/4 protein)
- 1 1/2tsp of each: Onion powder, basil, lemon juice
- 3tsp Parsley
- Pinch of each: Garlic salt, sea salt
- 4 1/2tsp Dill
- 3 Eggs (1/2 protein)
- 3oz total: Shredded cheddar cheese, parmesan cheese (full fat)

DIRECTIONS

1. Preheat oven to 375.
2. Lightly oil a large baking dish.
3. Dice green pepper, onion, garlic, and ham.
4. Add all vegetables to baking dish.
5. Top with diced ham.
6. In a separate bowl whisk, garlic, Greek yogurt, seasonings, and egg.
7. Pour yogurt mixture onto veggies and top with cheeses.
8. Cover and bake 1hr 30min or until vegetables are tender.

DIVIDE CASSEROLE INTO 3 SERVINGS

Weight loss Recipes
- no sugar, no flour, made deliciously easy -
WeightLossRecipesCookbook.com

Tuscan Pizza Casserole

servings: 3   cooking time: 1hr 30min

INGREDIENTS

- 3Lb 8oz total frozen: Asparagus, green beans, sweet onion, canned diced tomatoes, cauliflower (full vegetable)
- 6oz total: Spaghetti sauce, liquid from diced tomatoes
- 3Tbsp Minced garlic
- 6oz Cooked or canned chicken (1/2 protein)
- 3oz Turkey pepperoni (1/4 protein)
- 1Tbsp of each: Oregano, basil, parsley
- Pinch of each: Onion powder, garlic powder, garlic salt
- 3oz Cheddar or mozzarella cheese (full fat)

DIRECTIONS

1. Preheat oven to 375.
2. Pour half of spaghetti sauce and liquid from canned tomatoes into the bottom of a large baking dish.
3. Add asparagus, green beans, and cauliflower.
4. Top with remaining half of spaghetti sauce and tomato liquid.
5. Shred chicken.
6. Add chicken and minced garlic.
7. Top with seasonings and pepperoni.
8. Cover and bake 1hr 30min or until vegetables are tender.
9. Uncover and bake another 10min.

DIVIDE CASSEROLE INTO 3 SERVINGS

Weight loss Recipes
- no sugar, no flour, made deliciously easy -
WeightLossRecipesCookbook.com

Cheesy Tomato Soup

servings: 6   cooking time: 25min

INGREDIENTS

- 6lbs total: Onion, canned tomatoes
- 3lbs Vegetable broth
- 6Tbsp Tomato paste
- 7-10 Cloves garlic
- 6oz Shredded cheese
- 12oz Plain Greek yogurt
- 2Tbsp of each: Parsley, garlic salt, basil, onion powder, thyme

DIVIDE SOUP INTO 6 SERVINGS. SIDE EACH SERVING WITH 3/4 PROTEIN FOR A COMPLETE DINNER.

DIRECTIONS

1. Dice onion and garlic.
2. Heat and lightly oil a large pot.
3. Add onion and sauté 5-7min.
4. Add garlic and cook 1-2min longer.
5. Add tomatoes, broth, tomato paste, and seasonings.
6. Bring to a boil.
7. Reduce heat and simmer 12min.
8. Using a hand blender or work in batches using a blender, blend soup until smooth.
9. Return soup to pot.
10. Add cheese and mix until cheese is melted.
11. If cheese is not melted, return to a low heat, and stir until cheese melts.
12. Stir in Greek yogurt.

Weight loss Recipes
- no sugar, no flour, made deliciously easy -
WeightLossRecipesCookbook.com

Chicken Noodle Soup

servings: 6   cooking time: 27min

INGREDIENTS

- 3Lbs Vegetable or chicken broth
- 5 1/2lbs total: Celery, onion, frozen mixed vegetables, frozen carrots, frozen broccoli, palmini noodles
- 1tsp of each: Tarragon, thyme, rosemary
- 1/2tsp of each: Sea salt, ginger, turmeric, pepper
- 1Tbsp Minced garlic
- 24oz Cooked chicken

DIRECTIONS

1. Dice celery and onion.
2. Heat and lightly oil a large pot.
3. Sauté celery and onion 4-5min.
4. Add garlic and sauté 1-2min longer.
5. Shred chicken.
6. Add remaining ingredients to the pot and bring to a boil.
7. Reduce heat and simmer 15-20min or until vegetables are tender.

**DIVIDE SOUP INTO 6 SERVINGS.
SIDE EACH SERVING WITH A FAT
FOR A COMPLETE DINNER.**

Weight loss Recipes
- no sugar, no flour, made deliciously easy -
WeightLossRecipesCookbook.com

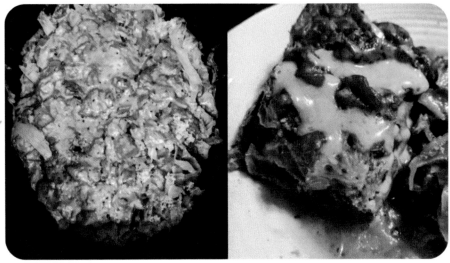

Slow Cooker Cabbage Lasagna

servings: 3   cooking time: 6hr

INGREDIENTS

- 2lb 7oz total: Cabbage, canned fire roasted tomato, onion (full vegetable)
- 6oz Ricotta cheese (1/2 protein)
- 6oz Shredded cheese (1/2 protein + full fat)
- 1Tbsp of each: Parsley, oregano, onion powder
- 1/2tsp Garlic powder
- 1 1/2oz Lemon juice
- 6oz Spaghetti sauce (condiment)

DIRECTIONS

1. Chop/shred cabbage.
2. Dice onion.
3. Pour and spread enough spaghetti sauce to cover the bottom of crock pot.
4. In a separate bowl mix ricotta, spaghetti sauce, spices, and lemon juice.
5. Layer 1/3 of each: Cabbage, onion, fire roasted tomatoes, ricotta mixture and cheese.
6. Repeat with remaining layers.
7. Cook on high 5-6hrs or until vegetables are tender.

DIVIDE LASAGNA INTO 3 SERVINGS

Weight loss Recipes
- no sugar, no flour, made deliciously easy -
WeightLossRecipesCookbook.com

91

Skinny Shepherd's Pie

servings: 2   cooking time: 1hr

INGREDIENTS

- 1 12oz Bag frozen cauliflower
- 18oz Frozen or cooked/roasted: Carrots, broccoli, peas
- 4oz Ricotta cheese (1/2 protein)
- 4oz Cooked turkey or chicken (1/2 protein)
- 2oz Shredded cheddar cheese (full fat)
- 3-4 Cloves garlic
- 1 Cup water
- 1tsp Season fry seasoning (find seasoning recipe in "Sauces, Seasonings, and Sides")
- Pinch of Sea salt

DIVIDE INTO 2 SERVINGS

DIRECTIONS

1. Preheat oven to 350.
2. Add frozen cauliflower, salt, and water to a pot.
3. Bring to a boil over high heat.
4. Reduce heat to med/low and simmer 10-12min or until cauliflower is tender.
5. Using a hand blender or blender, blend cauliflower and garlic until smooth.
6. Add ricotta, 1oz shredded cheese, seasonings, and mix.
7. Lightly oil a 8x8 or 10x8 baking dish.
8. Add vegetables except cauliflower mixture to baking dish.
9. Break/shred turkey into small pieces.
10. Sprinkle turkey on top of vegetables.
11. Add cauliflower mixture and spread evenly on top.
12. Cover and bake 1hr.
13. Top with 1oz cheese. Let sit 1-2min for cheese to melt.

Weight loss Recipes
- no sugar, no flour, made deliciously easy -
WeightLossRecipesCookbook.com

Cheeseburger Soup

servings: 6   cooking time: 50min

INGREDIENTS

- 12oz Cooked ground beef (1/2 protein)
- 12oz Ricotta cheese (1/2 protein)
- 6oz Shredded cheddar cheese (full fat)
- 6lbs total: 2 14oz Cans fire roasted tomatoes, cabbage, onion, celery, colored peppers, frozen corn, frozen carrots, frozen peas, frozen cauliflower
- 6-7 Cloves garlic
- 3lbs Vegetable broth
- 2Tbsp of each: Parsley, basil
- 1Tbsp of each: Cumin, paprika
- 2tsp of Garlic salt
- Pinch of Sea salt

DIVIDE INTO 6 SERVINGS

DIRECTIONS

1. Heat and lightly oil a large pot.
2. Slice and dice celery, onion, peppers, and cabbage.
3. Add diced vegetables to skillet and sauté 7-9min or until starting to brown.
4. Add remaining ingredients except shredded cheese to pot.
5. Bring to a boil.
6. Reduce heat and simmer 30-40min or until vegetables are tender.
7. Remove from heat and stir in cheese until melted

Weight loss Recipes
- no sugar, no flour, made deliciously easy -
WeightLossRecipesCookbook.com

Tuscan Onion Soup

servings: 6   cooking time: 25min

INGREDIENTS

- 3lbs Vegetable broth
- 6lbs total: Canned crushed tomatoes, canned diced tomatoes, canned fire roasted tomatoes, 6 small onions, spaghetti sauce
- 2Tbsp of each: Onion powder, garlic powder, basil, parsley, minced garlic
- 1tsp Garlic salt

DIRECTIONS

1. Heat and lightly oil a large pot.
2. Slice onions.
3. Add onions to pot and sauté until golden and tender.
4. Add garlic and cook another 1-2min.
5. Remove onions to weigh.
6. Add all ingredients to the pot and bring to a boil.
7. Reduce heat and simmer 12-15min.

**DIVIDE INTO 6 SERVINGS
SIDE EACH SERVING WITH A
PROTEIN AND A FAT FOR A
COMPLETE DINNER**

Weight loss Recipes
- no sugar, no flour, made deliciously easy -
WeightLossRecipesCookbook.com

The BEST Pot Roast

servings: 6-8   cooking time:- 6hr

INGREDIENTS

- 1 Beef roast
- Water
- Pinch of each: Garlic salt, thyme, rosemary
- 1Lb Carrots
- 3 Zucchini
- 2 Onions
- 1Tbsp Minced garlic

DIRECTIONS

1. Preheat oven to 350.
2. Add thawed roast to a large casserole dish and add about 1/4in water to dish.
3. Sprinkle roast with seasonings.
4. Cut carrots in half.
5. Cut zucchini into 4ths.
6. Slice onion.
7. Top roast with vegetables and sprinkle with more seasonings and minced garlic.
8. Cover and bake 5-6hrs.

WEIGH 4OZ MEAT AND 14OZ VEGETABLES
FOR EACH SERVNG AND SIDE EACH SERVING
WITH A FAT FOR A COMPLETE DINNER

Weight loss Recipes
- no sugar, no flour, made deliciously easy -
WeightLossRecipesCookbook.com

Instapot Pot Roast

servings: 6-8   cooking time:- 1hr

INGREDIENTS

- 1 Beef roast
- 1lb Carrots
- 3 Zucchini
- 3 Onions
- 1Tbsp of each: Worcestershire sauce, minced garlic
- 2Tbsp Soy sauce
- 1/2tsp Thyme
- Pinch of each: Parsley, sea salt, rosemary
- 1cup Broth

DIRECTIONS

1. Set instapot to sauté.
2. Sprinkle both sides of thawed roast with salt.
3. Sauté/sear roast 10min each side or until brown.
4. Remove roast and set aside.
5. Mix sauces, seasonings, and minced garlic.
6. Cut carrots into half.
7. Slice zucchini into 4ths.
8. Slice onion.
9. Add broth, and roast to instapot.
10. Pour sauce mixture over roast and top with vegetables.
11. Cover and pressure cook on high 30min.
12. Natural release 10min.

WEIGH 4OZ MEAT AND 14OZ VEGETABLES FOR EACH SERVNG AND SIDE EACH SERVING WITH A FAT FOR A COMPLETE DINNER

Weight loss Recipes
- no sugar, no flour, made deliciously easy -
WeightLossRecipesCookbook.com

Taco Ricotta Casserole

servings: 6   cooking time: 1hr 40min

INGREDIENTS

- 12oz Ricotta cheese
- 12oz Taco beef
- 2Tbsp Taco seasoning
- 6Tbsp Lime juice
- 6lbs total: Onion, cauliflower rice, green peppers, can Rotel, cabbage
- 12oz Liquid from Rotel
- 6oz Cheese

DIRECTIONS

1. Preheat oven to 375.
2. Mix ricotta, taco seasoning, lime juice, and Rotel liquid.
3. Add vegetables to a baking dish.
4. Top with taco beef, ricotta mixture and cheese.
5. Cover and bake 1hr 30min.
6. Uncover and bake 10min.

DIVIDE CASSEROLE INTO 6 SERVINGS

also find this recipe in my
volume 10 cookbook

Weight loss Recipes
- no sugar, no flour, made deliciously easy -
WeightLossRecipesCookbook.com

Broccoli Cheese Soup

servings: 6   cooking time: 25min

INGREDIENTS

- 6lbs total: Broccoli, carrots, onion
- 3lbs Vegetable broth
- 12oz Cheese
- 1lb 5oz Plain Greek yogurt
- 1Tbsp of each: Garlic powder, onion powder

DIRECTIONS

1. Dice onion.
2. Add onion to a large pot and sauté.
3. Add broth and vegetables to pot.
4. Bring to a boil.
5. Reduce heat and simmer 15-20min until broccoli is tender.
6. Add seasoning and cheese.
7. Stir until combined.
8. Stir in Greek yogurt.

DIVIDE CASSEROLE INTO 6 SERVINGS
also find this recipe in my
volume 11 cookbook

Weight loss Recipes
- no sugar, no flour, made deliciously easy -
WeightLossRecipesCookbook.com

Taco Supreme Casserole

servings: 4   cooking time: 1hr 45min

INGREDIENTS

- 8oz Cooked ground beef
- 6oz Canned black beans
- 2 Eggs
- 4oz Shredded cheddar cheese
- 4lbs total: Cabbage, onion, colored bell peppers, frozen broccoli, frozen corn, frozen carrots
- 8oz Salsa
- 1Tbsp of each: Minced garlic, taco seasoning

DIRECTIONS

1. Preheat oven to 375.
2. Pour a little salsa into the bottom of a large baking dish and tilt to coat the bottom.
3. Slice onion, cabbage, and peppers.
4. Mix cooked beef, eggs, black beans, 2oz cheese, minced garlic, and taco seasoning.
5. Add 2lbs of vegetables to casserole dish and top with half of beef mixture.
6. Add remaining vegetables and top with remaining beef mixture.
7. Sprinkle with 2oz cheese.
8. Cover and bake 1hr 45min or until vegetables are tender.

DIVIDE CASSEROLE INTO 4 SERVINGS

Weight loss Recipes
- no sugar, no flour, made deliciously easy -
WeightLossRecipesCookbook.com

Tex-mex Casserole

servings: 4   cooking time: 1hr 45min

INGREDIENTS

- 8oz Cooked ground beef
- 2 Eggs
- 4oz Shredded cheddar cheese
- 8oz Salsa
- 4lbs total: Onion, colored bell peppers, cabbage, frozen cauliflower, frozen corn, frozen carrots, frozen peas and carrots, frozen asparagus
- 1Tbsp of each: Minced garlic, taco seasoning

DIRECTIONS

1. Preheat oven to 375.
2. Pour a little salsa into the bottom of a large baking dish and tilt to coat the bottom. Slice onion, cabbage, and peppers.
3. Mix cooked beef, eggs, 2oz cheese, minced garlic, and taco seasoning.
4. Add 2lbs of vegetables to casserole dish and top with half of beef mixture.
5. Add remaining vegetables and top with remaining beef mixture.
6. Sprinkle with 2oz cheese.
7. Cover and bake 1hr 45min or until vegetables are tender.

DIVIDE CASSEROLE INTO 4 SERVINGS TOP/SIDE EACH SERVING WITH 1/4TH PROTEIN FOR A COMPLETE DINNER. (2OZ PLAIN GREEK YOGURT, 1/2OZ CHEESE, OR 1OZ RICOTTA CHEESE)

Weight loss Recipes
- no sugar, no flour, made deliciously easy -
WeightLossRecipesCookbook.com

100

Chicken Chili

servings: 7   cooking time: 50min

INGREDIENTS

- 14oz Cooked chicken
- 12oz Canned tri-colored beans (black beans, pinto beans, navy beans)
- Liquid from can of beans
- 4oz Shredded cheese
- 7oz Sour cream
- 7lbs total frozen: Cauliflower rice, spinach, onions and peppers, green beans, broccoli
- 2Tbsp Chili powder
- 1Tbsp Cumin
- 14oz Spaghetti sauce
- 2lbs Chicken broth

DIRECTIONS

1. Add all ingredients to a large pot and heat on high.
2. Bring to a boil.
3. Reduce heat to med/low and simmer 45min or until vegetables are tender.
4. Remove from heat and stir in cheese

DIVIDE SOUP INTO 7 CONTAINERS. TOP EACH CONTAINER WITH 1OZ SOUR CREAM.

Weight loss Recipes
- no sugar, no flour, made deliciously easy -
WeightLossRecipesCookbook.com

Bean Less Chili

servings: 4   cooking time: 3hr

INGREDIENTS

- 4lbs total: Cabbage, onion, celery, carrots, beets, green peppers
- 12oz Cooked ground beef
- 1/8cup Chili powder
- 1/2Tbsp of each: Cumin, garlic powder, onion powder
- 1Tbsp of each: Smoked paprika, oregano, minced garlic
- 2Lbs Chicken or vegetable broth
- 8oz Canned tomatoes
- 1/2tsp Allspice
- 1/8tsp Clove

DIRECTIONS

1. Heat and lightly oil a large pot.
2. Dice/slice onions, celery, and cabbage.
3. Add onions, celery, and cabbage to pot and sauté 10min.
4. Dice carrots into small pieces (or use frozen carrots) and add to pot.
5. Add minced garlic to pot and sauté 3-4min more.
6. Dice green peppers, beets (or use canned beets).
7. Add all ingredients to the pot.
8. Bring to a boil.
9. Cover, reduce heat, and simmer 1-3hrs or until vegetables are tender.

DIVIDE CHILI INTO 4 CONTAINERS.
TOP/SIDE EACH CONTAINER WITH A FAT
AND 1/4 PROTEIN FOR A COMPLETE DINNER.

Weight loss Recipes
- no sugar, no flour, made deliciously easy -
WeightLossRecipesCookbook.com

Chili

servings: 3   cooking time: 3hr

INGREDIENTS

- 6lbs total: Cabbage, onion, celery, carrots, beets, green peppers
- 12oz Cooked ground beef
- 7oz Canned tri-colored beans (black beans, navy beans, kidney beans)
- 2oz Liquid from canned beans
- 1/4cup Chili powder
- 1Tbsp of each: Cumin, onion powder, garlic power
- 2Tbsp of each: Smoked paprika, minced garlic, oregano.
- 3lbs Chicken or vegetable broth
- 12oz Canned tomatoes
- 1tsp All spice
- 1/4tsp Cloves

DIRECTIONS

1. Heat and lightly oil a large pot.
2. Dice/slice onions, celery, and cabbage.
3. Add onions, celery, and cabbage to pot and sauté 10min.
4. Dice carrots into small pieces (or use frozen carrots) and add to pot.
5. Add minced garlic to pot and sauté 3-4min more.
6. Dice green peppers, beets (or used canned beets).
7. Add all ingredients to the pot.
8. Bring to a boil.
9. Cover, reduce heat, and simmer 1-3hrs or until vegetables are tender.

DIVIDE CHILI INTO 6 CONTAINERS. TOP/SIDE EACH CONTAINER WITH A FAT AND 1/4 PROTEIN FOR A COMPLETE DINNER

Weight loss Recipes
- no sugar, no flour, made deliciously easy -
WeightLossRecipesCookbook.com

Vegetable Lasagna Soup

servings: 10   cooking time: 55min

INGREDIENTS

- 20oz Cooked ground beef
- 8oz Whole milk ricotta cheese
- 4oz Half and half
- 8oz Black olives
- 5Tbsp Minced garlic or 10 cloves garlic
- 3Tbsp of each: Garlic powder, onion powder, parsley, basil, balsamic vinegar
- 2Tbsp Oregano
- 1Tbsp of each: Thyme, rosemary
- 1tsp Turmeric
- 15oz Cooked chickpea pasta
- 20oz Canned diced tomatoes or spaghetti sauce
- 9lbs total: 4 onion, ½ stalk celery, 10oz bag frozen mushrooms, 3lb bag frozen cauliflower, 12oz bag frozen asparagus, 12oz bag frozen peas and carrots
- 4lbs Chicken or vegetable broth

DIRECTIONS

1. Heat and lightly oil a very large pot.
2. Dice onion and celery.
3. Add onion and celery to pot and sauté 4-5min or until tender.
4. Add minced garlic and cook another 1-2min.
5. Add all ingredients to pot except chickpea pasta and bring to a boil.
6. Reduce heat and simmer 30-45min stirring occasionally until vegetables are tender.
7. Cook chickpea pasta according to box directions.
8. Remove soup from heat and stir in cooked pasta

DIVIDE SOUP INTO 10 SERVINGS.
TOP/SIDE EACH SERVING WITH 1/4
PROTEIN FOR A COMPLETE DINNER.

Weight Loss Recipes
- no sugar, no flour, made deliciously easy -
WeightLossRecipesCookbook.com

Beef Stroganoff

servings: 10   cooking time: 30min

INGREDIENTS

- 4lbs Frozen cauliflower
- 6lbs total: 1 10oz bag frozen mushrooms, 1 12oz bag frozen zoodles, 1 12oz bag frozen carrots, 1/2 a stalk of celery, 1/2 a head of cabbage, 1 12oz bag frozen asparagus, 2 12oz bags frozen peas and carrots
- 20oz Cooked ground beef
- 4lbs Beef broth
- 7oz Sour cream
- 3oz Parmesan cheese
- 20oz Plain Greek yogurt
- 2Tbsp of each: Garlic powder, onion powder, parsley, minced garlic
- 2tsp of each: Smoked paprika, chili powder
- 1tsp of each: Sea salt, garlic salt
- 1/4cup Soy sauce

DIVIDE CAULIFLOWER MIXTURE INTO 10 CONTAINERS AND TOP EACH WITH CREAM MIXTURE. SIDE EACH SERVING WITH 1/4TH PROTEIN FOR A COMPLETE DINNER

DIRECTIONS

1. Add 2lbs broth, minced garlic, and cauliflower to a large pot.
2. Bring to a boil.
3. Cover and simmer 10-15min until tender.
4. Dice cabbage and celery.
5. Heat and lightly oil another large pot.
6. Add celery, cabbage, carrots, and mushrooms to pot and sauté 10min.
7. Add all vegetables to large pot and add 1lb broth.
8. In a separate bowl mix yogurt, 1lb broth, parmesan cheese, seasonings, and sour cream.
9. Add yogurt mixture, cooked ground beef, and soy sauce to cabbage mixture and heat on low until smoking but not boiling.
10. Using a hand blender or working in batches using a blender, blend cauliflower mixture until smooth.

Weight loss Recipes
- no sugar, no flour, made deliciously easy -
WeightLossRecipesCookbook.com

Red Bean Thai Peanut Bowl

servings: 7   cooking time: 25min

INGREDIENTS

- 7Lbs Frozen sugar snap pea stir fry (sugar snap pea, water chestnuts, broccoli, bell peppers, baby corn, mushrooms)
- 14oz Cooked ground beef
- 21oz Canned kidney beans (2 15.5oz cans)
- 1Tbsp of each: Onion powder, garlic powder, ginger, turmeric
- 1/4cup Soy sauce
- 3 1/2oz Peanut butter

DIRECTIONS

1. Add frozen veggies to a large pot.
2. Heat pot over high heat.
3. Sprinkle veggies with ginger, turmeric, and soy sauce.
4. Cook 10-15min stirring occasionally until veggies are tender.
5. Brown beef.
6. Add cooked beef, kidney beans (not drained), peanut butter, garlic powder, and onion powder, to a large bowl and mix.
7. Pour beef mixture into a skillet or saucepan and simmer 5-7min.

DIVIDE VEGETABLE INTO 7 CONTAINERS AND TOP EACH CONTAINER WITH BEEF MIXTURE.

Sauces, Seasonings, and Sides

Weight loss Recipes
- no sugar, no flour, made deliciously easy -
WeightLossRecipesCookbook.com

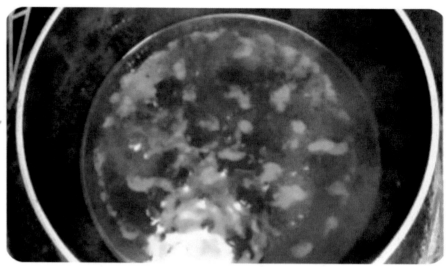

Enchilada sauce

servings: -   cooking time- 10-15min

INGREDIENTS

- 4Tbsp Chili powder
- 1/2tsp each: Garlic powder, sea salt
- 1/4tsp each: Cumin, oregano
- 2 cups Vegetable stock
- Avocado oil

DIRECTIONS

1. Lightly oil pan with avocado oil and heat over medium high heat.
2. Mix spices and add to heated pan.
3. Gradually add vegetable stock, whisk constantly to remove lumps.
4. Reduce heat, simmer 10-15 minutes until slightly thickened.

Weight loss Recipes
- no sugar, no flour, made deliciously easy -
WeightLossRecipesCookbook.com

Ranch Mockoritos

servings: -   cooking time- 7min

INGREDIENTS

- Colby cheese slices
- Ranch seasoning

DIRECTIONS

1. Preheat oven to 375.
2. Cut cheese slices into triangles.
3. Line a baking pan with parchment paper.
4. Place cheese slices on parchment paper and sprinkle with ranch seasoning.
5. Cook 5-7min or until desired crispiness.

SINGLE SERVING SIZE-
1oz = full fat
2oz = full protein

Weight loss Recipes
- no sugar, no flour, made deliciously easy -
WeightLossRecipesCookbook.com

Dijon Lemon Dipping Sauce

servings: -   cooking time: -

INGREDIENTS

- 1/2oz of each: Dijon mustard, lemon juice
- 1/4tsp Season Fry Seasoning (find seasoning recipe in "Sauces, Seasonings, and Sides")

DIRECTIONS

1. Add all ingredients to a small bowl
2. Mix

Weight loss Recipes
- no sugar, no flour, made deliciously easy -
WeightLossRecipesCookbook.com

Cranberry Pineapple Jam

servings: -   cooking time: 14min

INGREDIENTS

- Fresh or frozen pineapple
- Bagged fresh cranberries
- Orange zest

SINGLE SERVING SIZE-
6oz= full fruit

DIRECTIONS

1. Wash cranberries.
2. Add equal parts pineapple and cranberries to a pot.
3. Heat on high 3-4min.
4. Reduce heat to med and cook 10min until fruit starts to break down.
5. Stir in orange zest.
6. Let cool.
7. Refrigerate up to a week or freeze for longer storage.

Weight loss Recipes
- no sugar, no flour, made deliciously easy -
WeightLossRecipesCookbook.com

Orange Cranberry Jam

servings: -   cooking time: 10min

INGREDIENTS

- 12oz bag Cranberries
- 3 Oranges

SINGLE SERVING SIZE-
6oz = full fruit

DIRECTIONS

1. Wash 2 oranges and cranberries.
2. Pour cranberries into a medium pot.
3. Zest oranges.
4. Peel oranges and cut into smaller pieces.
5. Add oranges and zest to pot and heat over med/high heat.
6. Cook 10min stirring occasionally until fruit starts to breakdown.
7. If fruit starts to stick/burn to the bottom of pot, reduce heat to med.

Weight loss Recipes
- no sugar, no flour, made deliciously easy -
WeightLossRecipesCookbook.com

Homemade Salsa

servings: -   cooking time: 15min

INGREDIENTS

- 1 Anaheim pepper
- 1 Poblano pepper
- 3 Green bell peppers
- 1 Medium Sweet Vidalia onion
- 4-5 Cloves garlic
- 1/3cup Lime juice
- 1 Jalapeno pepper (optional)
- 6-8 Roma tomatoes
- Pinch of Sea salt

DIRECTIONS

1. Slice and core peppers removing the seeds and veins.
2. Peel onion and garlic.
3. Chop the end off the onion and slice into 4ths.
4. Add onion, peppers, and garlic to a food processor.
5. Pulse 7-10 times.
6. Add remaining ingredients and pulse until there are no longer large chunks.

SINGLE SERVING SIZE-
2oz = free condiment otherwise you can count this towards your vegetables.

Weight loss Recipes
- no sugar, no flour, made deliciously easy -
WeightLossRecipesCookbook.com

Avocado Fries

servings: -   cooking time- 20min

INGREDIENTS

- 3 Avocados
- 1Tbsp Nutritional yeast
- 2tsp Season fry seasoning (find seasoning recipe in "Sauces, Seasonings, and Sides")
- Sea salt

SINGLE SERVING SIZE-
   2oz = full fat

DIRECTIONS

1. Slice and peel avocados.
2. Sprinkle avocado slices with ½ of seasonings and nutritional yeast.
3. Flip and sprinkle with remaining seasonings.
4. Line an air fryer with parchment paper.
5. Air fry 400 for 15min flipping halfway or bake 400 for 15-20min flipping halfway.

Weight loss Recipes
- no sugar, no flour, made deliciously easy -
WeightLossRecipesCookbook.com

Homemade Tomato Sauce

servings: -   cooking time- 30min

INGREDIENTS

- 10-15 Roma tomatoes
- 2Tbsp Basil
- Sea salt
- 1-2Tbsp Minced garlic

DIRECTIONS

1. Dice tomatoes into medium chunks.
2. Add all ingredients to a large pot.
3. Heat over med heat.
4. Cook 15min or until mixture becomes saucy.
5. Reduce heat to low and cook another 15min.

SINGLE SERVING SIZE-
2oz = free condiment

Weight loss Recipes
- no sugar, no flour, made deliciously easy -
WeightLossRecipesCookbook.com

Berry Rhubarb Jam

servings: -   cooking time: 10min

INGREDIENTS

- Rhubarb
- Frozen berries
- Sea salt
- 1Tbsp Chia seeds

DIRECTIONS

1. Add equal parts of berries and rhubarb to a pot.
2. Sprinkle with sea salt.
3. Cook med/high 10min.
4. Remove from heat and mix in chia seeds.

SINGLE SERVING SIZE-
   6oz = full fruit

Find this recipe also in my Volume 4 cookbook and Cooking with Joy.

Weight loss Recipes
- no sugar, no flour, made deliciously easy -
WeightLossRecipesCookbook.com

Pineapple Rhubarb Jam

servings: -   cooking time: 10min

INGREDIENTS

- Rhubarb
- Pineapple
- Sea salt
- 1Tbsp Chia seeds

DIRECTIONS

1. Add equal parts of pineapple and rhubarb to a pot.
2. Sprinkle with sea salt.
3. Cook med/high 10min. Remove from heat and mix in chia seeds.

SINGLE SERVING SIZE-
    6oz = full fruit

Weight loss Recipes
- no sugar, no flour, made deliciously easy -
WeightLossRecipesCookbook.com

Fat Free Pesto

servings: -   cooking time:

INGREDIENTS

- Hand full of Basil leaves
- 1-2Tbsp Lemon juice
- 1 Clove garlic
- Pinch of Sea salt

DIRECTIONS

1. Add basil leaves to a bowl.
2. Add a splash of lemon juice, garlic, and salt.
3. Use a hand blender or blender and blend until smooth.

SINGLE SERVING SIZE–
2oz = condiment

Find this recipe also in my
Volume 13 cookbook

Sauces, Seasonings, and Sides

VEGETABLES & FRUITS

Baked Zucchini

servings: -   cooking time: 40min

INGREDIENTS

- Zucchini
- Spray olive oil
- Seasoned Fry Spice (find seasoning recipe in "Sauces, Seasonings, and Sides")
- Sea salt

DIRECTIONS

1. Slice zucchini thin.
2. Sprinkle with sea salt and let sit 10min to release water.
3. Preheat oven to 350.
4. Spray baking sheet with olive oil.
5. Pour excess liquid off of zucchinis and layer on baking sheet.
6. Sprinkle with seasoning
7. Bake 20-30min or until golden brown but not burnt.

SINGLE SERVING SIZE-
6oz = full lunch vegetables
14oz = full dinner vegetables

Weight loss Recipes
- no sugar, no flour, made deliciously easy -
WeightLossRecipesCookbook.com

Basil Refrigerator Pickles

servings: -   cooking time: -

INGREDIENTS

- 7-10 leaves Fresh basil
- 2-3 Cucumbers
- 1tsp Sea salt
- 1-2cups total: Apple cider vinegar, white wine vinegar

DIRECTIONS

1. Slice cucumbers.
2. Dice basil.
3. Add all ingredients except vinegar to a jar
4. Add vinegar to cover cucumbers.
5. Refrigerate overnight for best flavor.

SINGLE SERVING SIZE-
2oz = free condiment otherwise you can count this towards your vegetables.

Weight loss Recipes
- no sugar, no flour, made deliciously easy -
WeightLossRecipesCookbook.com

Air Fried Crispy Onions

servings: -   cooking time: 20min

INGREDIENTS

- 1 Vidalia onion
- 2tsp Seasoned Fry Seasoning (find seasoning recipe in "Sauces, Seasonings, and Sides")
- Spray olive oil

DIRECTIONS

1. Slice onions.
2. Add onions to a bowl.
3. Spray with olive oil.
4. Add seasoning and toss to coat onions.
5. Place onion in air fryer and cook 390 for 15-20min stirring occasionally or until desired crispiness.

SINGLE SERVING SIZE-
6oz = full lunch vegetables
14oz = full dinner vegetables

Weight loss Recipes
- no sugar, no flour, made deliciously easy -
WeightLossRecipesCookbook.com

Air Fryer Zucchini Fries

servings: -   cooking time: 40min

INGREDIENTS

- Zucchini
- Spray olive oil
- Seasoned Fry Seasoning (find seasoning recipe in "Sauces, Seasonings, and Sides")

DIRECTIONS

1. Cut zucchini into 8ths or fry shape.
2. Place in a large bowl.
3. Spray with olive oil and sprinkle with seasoning.
4. Toss to evenly coat fries.
5. Place fries in air fryer and cook 390 for 30-40min stirring occasionally or until desired crispiness.

SINGLE SERVING SIZE-
   6oz = full lunch vegetables
   14oz = full dinner vegetables

Weight loss Recipes
- no sugar, no flour, made deliciously easy -
WeightLossRecipesCookbook.com

Air Fried Radish Taters

servings: -   cooking time: 30min

INGREDIENTS	DIRECTIONS
• 1 bag Radish • 2tsp Seasoned Fry Seasoning (find seasoning recipe in "Sauces, Seasonings, and Sides")	1. Slice radishes in half. 2. Lightly spray with olive oil. 3. Add seasoning and mix. 4. Place in air fryer and cook 390 for 30min stirring occasionally.

SINGLE SERVING SIZE-
   6oz = full lunch vegetables
   14oz = full dinner vegetables

Weight loss Recipes
- no sugar, no flour, made deliciously easy -
WeightLossRecipesCookbook.com

Crispy Air Fried Cabbage

servings: -   cooking time: 30min

INGREDIENTS

- Cabbage
- 1tsp of each: Cumin, onion powder
- 1/2tsp Garlic salt

DIRECTIONS

1. Slice cabbage into small pieces
2. Add cabbage to a bowl and sprinkle with seasonings.
3. Toss/stir.
4. Line air fryer with parchment paper.
5. Place in air fryer and cook 390 for 30min stirring halfway.

SINGLE SERVING SIZE-
   6oz = full lunch vegetables
   14oz = full dinner vegetables

Weight loss Recipes
- no sugar, no flour, made deliciously easy -
WeightLossRecipesCookbook.com

Chipotle Eggplant Fries

servings: -   cooking time: 40min

INGREDIENTS

- 1-2 Eggplants
- Chipotle seasoning (find seasoning recipe in "Sauces, Seasonings, and Sides")

DIRECTIONS

1. Preheat oven to 375.
2. Cut eggplant into matchsticks.
3. Lightly spray or drizzle with olive oil and sprinkle with chipotle seasoning.
4. Toss to coat fries evenly.
5. Lightly oil a baking pan.
6. Place fries on pan and cook 30-40min or until desired crispiness.

SINGLE SERVING SIZE-
   6oz = full lunch vegetables
   14oz = full dinner vegetables

Weight loss Recipes
- no sugar, no flour, made deliciously easy -
WeightLossRecipesCookbook.com

Cauli Rice Veggie Wok

servings: -   cooking time: 15min

INGREDIENTS

- 3 12oz bags Frozen cauliflower rice
- 3 12oz bags Frozen vegetable stir fry blend
- 1tsp Ginger
- Soy sauce
- Toasted sesame oil
- 2tsp Onion powder
- Pinch of each: Sea salt, curry powder
- 4-5 Cloves garlic

DIRECTIONS

1. Heat a wok or a large pot over medium high heat and lightly oil with sesame oil.
2. Add frozen vegetables.
3. Dice garlic.
4. Add seasonings and garlic to pot and cook 10-15min or until vegetables are tender.
5. Stir occasionally to prevent burning.
6. Add desired amount of vegetables to plate (6oz for lunch or 14oz for dinner)
7. Lightly drizzle with soy sauce.

SINGLE SERVING SIZE-
6oz = full lunch vegetables
14oz = full dinner vegetables

Weight loss Recipes
- no sugar, no flour, made deliciously easy -
WeightLossRecipesCookbook.com

Parsnip Air Fryer
Cheesy Fries

servings: -   cooking time: 40min

INGREDIENTS

- Parsnips
- Nutritional yeast
- Sea salt

DIRECTIONS

1. Slice parsnips into thin matchsticks.
2. Lightly spray with olive oil and sprinkle with nutritional yeast and salt.
3. Toss/mix to coat fries.
4. Air fry 390 for 40min.
5. Stir occasionally for even cooking.

SINGLE SERVING SIZE-
   6oz = full lunch vegetables
   14oz = full dinner vegetables

Weight loss Recipes
- no sugar, no flour, made deliciously easy -
WeightLossRecipesCookbook.com

126

Crispy Hot Cauli Wings

servings: -   cooking time: 40min

INGREDIENTS

- 2 12oz bag Frozen cauliflower
- 1Tbsp Franks hot sauce
- 1/2tsp of each: Onion powder, paprika, nutritional yeast
- Sea salt

DIRECTIONS

1. Add frozen cauliflower to a large bowl.
2. Add hot sauce, seasonings, and mix.
3. Place cauliflower in an air fryer and cook 390 20min.
4. Stir/toss and cook another 20min.
5. Repeat until desired crispiness.
6. Or bake 400 15min.
7. Stir and repeat until desired crispiness.

SINGLE SERVING SIZE-
   6oz = full lunch vegetables
   14oz = full dinner vegetables

Weight loss Recipes
- no sugar, no flour, made deliciously easy -
WeightLossRecipesCookbook.com

BBQ Air Fryer Cauliflower

servings: -   cooking time: 45min

INGREDIENTS

- 2 12oz Frozen bags cauliflower
- 2Tbsp Sugar free BBQ sauce
- Pinch of each: Garlic salt, paprika, onion powder

DIRECTIONS

1. Add all ingredients to a bowl and toss/mix to evenly coat frozen cauliflower.
2. Pour cauliflower into an air fryer and cook 390 for 30min.
3. Stir and cook another 10-15min or until desired crispiness.

SINGLE SERVING SIZE-
6oz = full lunch vegetables
14oz = full dinner vegetables

Cinnamon Refried Squash

servings: -   cooking time: 45min

INGREDIENTS

- 2 Roasted Hubbard squash
- 2tsp Cinnamon
- 1/2cup Vegetable broth
- 1/4tsp Sea salt

DIRECTIONS

1. Preheat oven to 350.
2. Scrape squash from skins and place in a medium baking dish.
3. In a separate bowl mix cinnamon, salt, and broth.
4. Pour cinnamon mixture over squash.
5. Cover and bake 45min.

SINGLE SERVING SIZE-
6oz = full lunch vegetables
14oz = full dinner vegetables

Weight loss Recipes
- no sugar, no flour, made deliciously easy -
WeightLossRecipesCookbook.com

Air Fryer Carrot Chips

servings: -   cooking time: 30min

INGREDIENTS

- 1 Bag Crinkle cut carrots (weigh after cooking)
- 2tsp Season fry seasoning (find seasoning recipe in "Sauces, Seasonings, and Sides")
- 1tsp Nutritional yeast

DIRECTIONS

1. Add carrots to a large bowl and lightly spray with oil.
2. Add seasonings and mix.
3. Add carrots to air fryer and cook 390 for 30min.
4. Stir halfway for even cooking.

SINGLE SERVING SIZE-
6oz = full lunch vegetables
14oz = full dinner vegetables

Weight loss Recipes
- no sugar, no flour, made deliciously easy -
WeightLossRecipesCookbook.com

Carrot Buffalo Crisps

servings: -   cooking time: 50min

INGREDIENTS

- 1 Bag Crinkle cut raw carrots
- 1Tbsp Franks hot sauce
- 1/2tsp Onion powder
- Pinch of each: Garlic salt, pepper

DIRECTIONS

1. Mix/toss all ingredients together to evenly coat.
2. Place carrots in an air fryer and cook 390 for 45-50min or until desired crispiness.
3. Stir once or twice for even cooking.

SINGLE SERVING SIZE-
6oz = full lunch vegetables
14oz = full dinner vegetables

Weight loss Recipes
- no sugar, no flour, made deliciously easy -
WeightLossRecipesCookbook.com

Buffalo Eggplant Fries

servings: -   cooking time: 30min

INGREDIENTS

- 1 Small eggplant
- 1Tbsp of each: Nutritional yeast, franks hot sauce
- 2tsp Season fry seasoning (find seasoning recipe in "Sauces, Seasonings, and Sides")

DIRECTIONS

1. Slice eggplant into matchsticks/fries.
2. Add remaining seasonings and sauces to a large bowl.
3. Toss to evenly coat.
4. Add fries to air fryer and cook 390 for 25-30min.
5. Stir halfway for even roasting.

SINGLE SERVING SIZE-
6oz = full lunch vegetables
14oz = full dinner vegetables

Weight loss Recipes
- no sugar, no flour, made deliciously easy -
WeightLossRecipesCookbook.com

Fried Zucchini

servings: -   cooking time: 30min

INGREDIENTS

- 1-2 Zucchini

DIRECTIONS

1. Heat and lightly oil a griddle or skillet.
2. Slice zucchini.
3. Place zucchini slices on griddle and cook 3-4min.
4. Flip and cook another 3-4min.
5. Repeat until desired doneness.

SINGLE SERVING SIZE-
   6oz = full lunch vegetables
   14oz = full dinner vegetables

Weight loss Recipes
- no sugar, no flour, made deliciously easy -
WeightLossRecipesCookbook.com

Cinnamon Air Fried Carrot Crisps

servings: -   cooking time- 20min

INGREDIENTS

- 1 Bag crinkle cut carrots
- 1tsp Cinnamon
- Pinch of Sea salt

DIRECTIONS

1. Line an air fryer with parchment paper.
2. Add carrots to lines air fryer and sprinkle with seasonings.
3. Cook 390 for 15-20min.
4. Stir halfway for even roasting.

SINGLE SERVING SIZE-
6oz = full lunch vegetables
14oz = full dinner vegetables

134

Weight loss Recipes
- no sugar, no flour, made deliciously easy -
WeightLossRecipesCookbook.com

Ginger Curry Stir Fry

servings: -   cooking time- 35min

INGREDIENTS

- 3 12oz bags Frozen cauliflower rice
- 1 12oz bag Frozen green beans
- 1 12oz bag Frozen zucchini
- 1 Vidalia onion
- 1tsp of each: Curry powder, onion powder
- 1/2tsp of each: Sea salt, turmeric powder
- 4-5 cloves Garlic
- Toasted sesame oil

DIRECTIONS

1. Heat and lightly oil a wok or large pot with the sesame oil.
2. Slice onion.
3. Mince garlic.
4. Add frozen vegetables to wok and top with seasoning.
5. Cook and stir occasionally 30-35min or until vegetables are tender.

SINGLE SERVING SIZE-
6oz = full lunch vegetables
14oz = full dinner vegetables

Weight loss Recipes
- no sugar, no flour, made deliciously easy -
WeightLossRecipesCookbook.com

Cauliflower Ranch Stir Fry

servings: -   cooking time- 30min

INGREDIENTS
- 2 12oz Bags frozen cauliflower rice
- 1 12oz Bag frozen of each: carrots, green beans, peas
- 1 10oz Bag frozen zucchini
- 1 Medium onion
- 4-5 Cloves garlic
- 1Tbsp of each: Onion powder, garlic powder, dill, parsley
- 1tsp Garlic salt

DIRECTIONS
1. Heat and lightly oil a wok or large skillet over med/high.
2. Slice/dice onion and garlic.
3. Add frozen veggies and cook 10min.
4. Add seasonings and stir.
5. Cook 20-30min or until vegetables are tender and starting to brown.

SINGLE SERVING SIZE-
6oz = full lunch vegetables
14oz = full dinner vegetables

Weight loss Recipes
- no sugar, no flour, made deliciously easy -
WeightLossRecipesCookbook.com

Cheese Less Cheesy
Carrot Fries

servings: -   cooking time- 20min

INGREDIENTS

- Baby carrots
- 1tsp Chipotle seasoning (find seasoning recipe in "Sauces, Seasonings, and Sides")
- 1Tbsp Nutritional yeast

DIRECTIONS

1. Line an air fryer with parchment paper.
2. Add carrots to a large bowl and add seasonings and a tiny drizzle of olive oil.
3. Toss to coat carrots.
4. Add carrots to air fryer and cook 400 for 15-20min or until desired crispiness.
5. Stir halfway for even roasting.

SINGLE SERVING SIZE-
6oz = full lunch vegetables
14oz = full dinner vegetables

Weight loss Recipes
- no sugar, no flour, made deliciously easy -
WeightLossRecipesCookbook.com

Creamy Cauliflower Mashed Potatoes

servings: -   cooking time- 15min

INGREDIENTS

- 6 12oz bags Frozen cauliflower
- 4cups Vegetable broth
- 5-6 Cloves garlic

DIRECTIONS

1. Add broth and cauliflower to a large pot.
2. Cover and bring to a boil.
3. Stir occasionally to prevent burning.
4. Reduce heat to med/high and cook 12min or until cauliflower is tender and falling apart.
5. Remove from heat.
6. Mince garlic and add to pot.
7. Using a hand blender or blender, blend until smooth.

SINGLE SERVING SIZE-
6oz = full lunch vegetables
14oz = full dinner vegetables
You can add 1-2oz extra for the broth

Weight loss Recipes
- no sugar, no flour, made deliciously easy -
WeightLossRecipesCookbook.com

138

Cheese Less Cheesy Cabbage

servings: -   cooking time- 20min

INGREDIENTS

- 1 Small head cabbage
- 1/2tsp Sea salt
- 2Tbsp Nutritional yeast

DIRECTIONS

1. Slice cabbage.
2. Add cabbage to a large bowl and lightly drizzle with oil.
3. Add spices and mix. Line an air fryer with parchment paper.
4. Add cabbage and cook 390 for 15-20min or until desired crispiness.
5. Stir halfway for even roasting.
6. Or roast in an oven 400 for 15-20min.

SINGLE SERVING SIZE-
6oz = full lunch vegetables
14oz = full dinner vegetables

Weight loss Recipes
- no sugar, no flour, made deliciously easy -
WeightLossRecipesCookbook.com

139

Ranch Roasted Cauliflower Bites

servings: -   cooking time- 20min

INGREDIENTS

- 2 12oz Bags frozen cauliflower
- 1Tbsp Ranch seasoning (find seasoning recipe in "Sauces, Seasonings, and Sides")
- Pinch of Sea salt
- Optional – 2tsp Nutritional yeast

DIRECTIONS

1. Add frozen cauliflower to a bowl and toss with seasonings.
2. Line an air fryer with parchment paper.
3. Add cauliflower and air fry 400 for 20min stirring halfway for even roasting.
4. Or roast in an oven 400 for 20-30min stirring every 10min until desired crispiness.

SINGLE SERVING SIZE-
   6oz = full lunch vegetables
   14oz = full dinner vegetables

Cheesy Roasted Radishes

servings: -   cooking time- 20min

INGREDIENTS

- 1 Bag Radishes
- 1Tbsp Nutritional yeast
- 1/2tsp Chipotle seasoning or season fry seasoning (find seasoning recipes in "Sauces, Seasonings, and Sides")
- Sea salt

DIRECTIONS

1. Slice radishes in half.
2. Line an air fryer with parchment paper or preheat oven to 400.
3. Add radishes to air fryer and sprinkle with seasonings.
4. Mix to evenly coat.
5. Air fry 400 for 20min, flip halfway for even roasting or bake 400 for 20-30min stirring halfway.

SINGLE SERVING SIZE-
   6oz = full lunch vegetables
   14oz = full dinner vegetables

Tomato Basil Carrot Fries

servings: -   cooking time- 20min

INGREDIENTS

- 1 Bag baby carrots
- 1oz Balsamic vinegar
- 2oz Spaghetti sauce (condiment up to 2oz free)
- 1tsp Nutritional yeast
- Pinch of Basil

DIRECTIONS

1. Add all ingredients to a small pan and mix.
2. Place pan in an air fryer and cook 400 for 20min.
3. Stir halfway for even roasting.
4. Or bake 400 30-40min stirring 1-2 times for even roasting.

SINGLE SERVING SIZE-
6oz = full lunch vegetables
14oz = full dinner vegetables

Weight loss Recipes
- no sugar, no flour, made deliciously easy -
WeightLossRecipesCookbook.com

142

Zucchini Chips

servings: -   cooking time- 25min

INGREDIENTS

- 1 Medium Zucchini
- Season Fry Seasoning (find seasoning recipe in "Sauces, Seasonings, and Sides")
- Nutritional Yeast

DIRECTIONS

1. Slice zucchini into thin chips.
2. Toss zucchini in seasonings.
3. Line an air fryer with parchment paper and layer zucchini into one flat layer.
4. Cook 400 for 25min flipping halfway for even cooking.
5. Or bake 375 for 35-45min.

SINGLE SERVING SIZE-
6oz = full lunch vegetables
14oz = full dinner vegetables

Chili Cheese Carrot Fries

servings: -   cooking time- 30min

INGREDIENTS

- 2 Bags of Petite carrots
- Chili powder
- Nutritional yeast
- Sea salt

DIRECTIONS

1. Add carrots to a large bowl.
2. Liberally sprinkle with chili powder and nutritional yeast.
3. Sprinkle with sea salt and stir.
4. Line an air fryer with parchment paper and air fry 400 for 25-30min.
5. Stir halfway for even roasting.
6. Or bake 375 for 45-40min stirring occasionally.

SINGLE SERVING SIZE-
6oz = full lunch vegetables
14oz = full dinner vegetables

Weight Loss Recipes
- no sugar, no flour, made deliciously easy -
WeightLossRecipesCookbook.com

Asian Air Fried Salad

servings: -   cooking time- 20min

INGREDIENTS

- 1 Hand full spring mix lettuce
- 1/2cup of each: Broccoli, carrot chips, coleslaw mix, celery
- 1 Green pepper
- 2Tbsp of each: Nutritional yeast, soy sauce
- 3Tbsp Oriental seasoning (find seasoning recipe in "Sauces, Seasonings, and Sides")

DIRECTIONS

1. Dice celery and green pepper.
2. Add all ingredients to a large bowl and mix.
3. Line an air fryer with parchment paper.
4. Add vegetables to air fryer and cook 400 for 20min.
5. Stir halfway for even cooking.
6. Or bake 375 for 30min stirring halfway.

SINGLE SERVING SIZE-
6oz = full lunch vegetables
14oz = full dinner vegetables

Weight loss Recipes
- no sugar, no flour, made deliciously easy -
WeightLossRecipesCookbook.com

Cheesy Air Fried Green Tomatoes

servings: -   cooking time- 30min

INGREDIENTS

- 10-20 Green tomatoes
- 2Tbsp Nutritional yeast
- 2tsp Chipotle seasoning (find seasoning recipe in "Sauces, Seasonings, and Sides")
- 1tsp Sea salt

DIRECTIONS

1. Slice tomatoes.
2. Lightly oil a small pan or line an air fryer with parchment paper.
3. Sprinkle tomatoes with seasonings and lightly stir.
4. Air fry 400 for 30min.
5. Stir halfway for even roasting.
6. Or bake 375 for 45-50min flipping halfway.

SINGLE SERVING SIZE-
6oz = full lunch vegetables
14oz = full dinner vegetables

Weight loss Recipes
- no sugar, no flour, made deliciously easy -
WeightLossRecipesCookbook.com

Air Fried Mushrooms

servings: -   cooking time- 15min

INGREDIENTS

- 1 Package Sliced white mushrooms
- 2tsp Nutritional yeast
- Pinch of Sea salt

DIRECTIONS

1. Wash mushrooms.
2. Lightly oil a small baking pan that fits inside an air fryer or line air fryer with parchment paper.
3. Add mushrooms to pan and toss/mix with seasonings.
4. Air fry 400 for 15min stirring halfway for even roasting.
5. Or bake 375 for 45-50min stirring halfway.

SINGLE SERVING SIZE-
   6oz = full lunch vegetables
   14oz = full dinner vegetables

Weight loss Recipes
- no sugar, no flour, made deliciously easy -
WeightLossRecipesCookbook.com

Garlic Balsamic Roasted Mushrooms

servings: -   cooking time- 35min

INGREDIENTS

- 8oz Package white mushrooms (weigh after cooking)
- 1Tbsp of each: Soy sauce, minced garlic
- 2Tbsp Balsamic vinegar
- 1/2tsp Thyme
- Pinch of Sea salt

DIRECTIONS

1. Preheat oven to 375.
2. Line a baking pan with parchment paper.
3. Wash mushrooms.
4. Sprinkle and drizzle mushrooms with seasonings and sauces.
5. Bake 30-35min.
6. Stir halfway for even roasting

SINGLE SERVING SIZE-
   6oz = full lunch vegetables
   14oz = full dinner vegetables

Weight loss Recipes
- no sugar, no flour, made deliciously easy -
WeightLossRecipesCookbook.com

Crispy Squash Chips

servings: -   cooking time- 30min

INGREDIENTS

- Squash rinds
- Chipotle seasoning (find seasoning recipe in "Sauces, Seasonings, and Sides")
- Nutritional yeast

DIRECTIONS

1. Preheat oven to 400.
2. Wash and peel squash.
3. Lightly oil a baking pan and place squash peelings on pan.
4. Sprinkle with seasonings.
5. Bake 30min or until golden and crispy.
6. Stir 2-3 times for even roasting.

SINGLE SERVING SIZE-
   6oz = full lunch vegetables
   14oz = full dinner vegetables

Weight loss Recipes
- no sugar, no flour, made deliciously easy -
WeightLossRecipesCookbook.com

149

Asian Roasted Cabbage

servings: -   cooking time- 40min

INGREDIENTS

- Cabbage
- Soy sauce
- Oriental Seasoning (find seasoning recipe in "Sauces, Seasonings, and Sides")
- Nutritional yeast
- Everything But The Bagel Seasoning

DIRECTIONS

1. Preheat oven to 375.
2. Line a baking pan with parchment paper.
3. Slice cabbage thin.
4. Add cabbage to lined baking pan and drizzle with soy sauce and sprinkle with seasonings.
5. Roast 35-40min stirring occasionally until golden.

SINGLE SERVING SIZE-
6oz = full lunch vegetables
14oz = full dinner vegetables

Balsamic Rosemary Roasted Radish Taters

servings: -   cooking time- 30min

INGREDIENTS

- 16oz Radish
- 1Tbsp of each: Balsamic vinegar, nutritional yeast, rosemary
- Pinch of Sea salt

DIRECTIONS

1. Slice radishes in half.
2. Add all ingredients to a bowl and mix to evenly coat radishes.
3. Line an air fryer or a baking pan with parchment paper.
4. Air fry 400-430 for 25-30min stirring halfway or until desired crispiness.
5. Or bake 400 for 35-40min stirring occasionally for even roasting.

SINGLE SERVING SIZE-
6oz = full lunch vegetables
14oz = full dinner vegetables

Weight loss Recipes
- no sugar, no flour, made deliciously easy -
WeightLossRecipesCookbook.com

Grilled Seasoned Vegetables

servings: -   cooking time- 30min

INGREDIENTS

- Zucchini, eggplant, onion, pickles, carrots, brussels sprouts, radish
- Greek seasoning (find seasoning recipe in "Sauces, Seasonings, and Sides")
- Sea salt
- Olive oil

DIRECTIONS

1. Heat and lightly oil grill to med/high heat (Add hickory wood chips for a smokey flavor).
2. Slice zucchini, eggplant, and onion.
3. Sprinkle zucchini and eggplant with salt and let sit to expel water.
4. Lightly spray or drizzle vegetables with olive oil, and sprinkle with Greek seasoning.
5. Grill vegetables 5-10min each side until golden brown.

SINGLE SERVING SIZE-
   6oz = full lunch vegetables
   14oz = full dinner vegetables

Weight loss Recipes
- no sugar, no flour, made deliciously easy -
WeightLossRecipesCookbook.com

152

Grilled Vegetables

servings: -   cooking time- 30min

INGREDIENTS

- Raw chicken breast
- Fat free pesto (find pesto recipe in "Sauces, Seasonings, and Sides")
- Sea salt
- Spray olive oil

DIRECTIONS

1. Heat grill to medium/high heat.
2. Spray chicken breast with olive oil and sprinkle with salt.
3. Grill chicken 10-15min each side.
4. Brush/rub chicken with pesto and grill 5min each side.
5. Cook until internal temp reaches 160.

SINGLE SERVING SIZE-
   6oz = full lunch vegetables
   14oz = full dinner vegetables

Weight loss Recipes
- no sugar, no flour, made deliciously easy -
WeightLossRecipesCookbook.com

Garlic Dill Refrigerator Cucumbers

servings: -   cooking time-

INGREDIENTS

- Cucumbers
- Onion
- Pinch of each: Garlic salt, dill
- Apple cider vinegar
- White wine vinegar

DIRECTIONS

1. Slice cucumbers very thin.
2. Add cucumbers to a bowl.
3. Pour in apple cider vinegar to almost cover cucumbers, add white wine vinegar until cucumbers are covered.
4. Add seasonings and refrigerate overnight.

Find this recipe also in my Volume 10 cookbook and Cooking with Joy 2.

SINGLE SERVING SIZE-
6oz = full lunch vegetables
14oz = full dinner vegetables

Weight loss Recipes
- no sugar, no flour, made deliciously easy -
WeightLossRecipesCookbook.com

Crockpot Apples and Spice

servings: -   cooking time: 6hr

INGREDIENTS

- 6lbs Apple
- 4Tbsp Cinnamon
- 2Tbsp Maple extract
- 1/2tsp of each: Nutmeg, instant coffee

DIRECTIONS

1. Dice apples.
2. Add apples and seasonings to crockpot and mix.
3. Cook on high 4-6hrs or until apples start to breakdown.

SINGLE SERVING SIZE-
    6oz= full fruit

Weight loss Recipes
- no sugar, no flour, made deliciously easy -
WeightLossRecipesCookbook.com

Cinnamon Air Fried Fruit

servings: -   cooking time: 20min

INGREDIENTS

- Pineapple
- Papaya
- Mango
- Cinnamon
- Sea salt

DIRECTIONS

1. Line an air fryer with parchment paper.
2. Add fruit and sprinkle with cinnamon and salt.
3. Air fry 390 for 20min or until desired crispiness.

SINGLE SERVING SIZE-
    6oz = full fruit

Weight loss Recipes
- no sugar, no flour, made deliciously easy -
WeightLossRecipesCookbook.com

Coffee Air Fried Apples and Banana

servings: -   cooking time: 20min

INGREDIENTS

- 1 Apple
- 1 Banana
- Cinnamon
- Instant coffee
- Sea salt

DIRECTIONS

1. Line an air fryer with parchment paper.
2. Slice banana and apple.
3. Layer fruit in the lined air fryer.
4. Liberally sprinkle with seasonings.
5. Air fry 390 for 20min

SINGLE SERVING SIZE-
    6oz = full fruit

Weight loss Recipes
- no sugar, no flour, made deliciously easy -
WeightLossRecipesCookbook.com

Air Fried Grapes

servings: -   cooking time: 20min

INGREDIENTS

- Grapes

DIRECTIONS

1. Line an air fryer with parchment paper and add grapes.
2. Air fry 390 for 15-20min or until desired doneness.

SINGLE SERVING SIZE-
   6oz = full fruit

Weight loss Recipes
- no sugar, no flour, made deliciously easy -
WeightLossRecipesCookbook.com

Cinnamon Air Fried Apples

servings: -   cooking time: 15min

INGREDIENTS

- Apples
- Cinnamon
- Sea salt

DIRECTIONS

1. Slice apples.
2. Toss apple slices in cinnamon and sea salt.
3. Place in air fryer and cook 390 for 10-15min or until desired crispiness.

SINGLE SERVING SIZE-
   6oz = full fruit

Sauces, Seasonings, and Sides

MEATS
&
PROTEINS

Weight loss Recipes
- no sugar, no flour, made deliciously easy -
WeightLossRecipesCookbook.com

Cheesy
Chicken Nuggets

servings: 4   cooking time: 12 min

INGREDIENTS

- 16oz Canned chicken
- 4oz Shredded cheese
- Nutritional yeast
- Chipotle seasoning (find seasoning recipe in "Sauces, Seasonings, and Sides")

DIRECTIONS

1. Line an air fryer with parchment paper or preheat oven to 375 and line a baking pan with parchment paper.
2. Mix chicken and shredded cheese.
3. Using your hands, squish and mold chicken mixture into nugget size balls.
4. Place in lined air fryer and sprinkle with seasonings.
5. Air fry 400 for 12min or bake 35-40min.
6. Flip halfway and sprinkle with more seasonings.

SINGLE SERVING SIZE-
5oz nuggets = full protein and full fat

Weight loss Recipes
- no sugar, no flour, made deliciously easy -
WeightLossRecipesCookbook.com

Rosemary Balsamic Fried Chicken

servings: -   cooking time: 15min

INGREDIENTS

- 3 Packages of chicken breast (9 chicken breast or as many as want)
- Balsamic vinegar
- Sea salt
- Dried rosemary

DIRECTIONS

1. Remove chicken from packages and place in a Tupperware.
2. Drizzle with balsamic and sprinkle with seasonings.
3. Flip and repeat with other side.
4. Refrigerate 30min to marinate.
5. Heat and lightly oil a skillet to med/high heat.
6. Add chicken breast and cover.
7. Cook 3-5min each side.
8. Repeat flipping and cooking until internal temp reaches 180.
9. Remove from skillet and let sit 1min before serving.
10. Repeat with any remaining chicken breast.

SINGLE SERVING SIZE-
   4oz = full protein

Weight loss Recipes
- no sugar, no flour, made deliciously easy -
WeightLossRecipesCookbook.com

Seasoned Grilled Chicken

servings: -   cooking time: 15min

INGREDIENTS

- 4-6 Raw chicken breast
- 2Tbsp Olive oil
- 1Tbsp Paprika
- 2tsp of each: Sea salt, chili powder, onion powder, garlic powder
- 1tsp Thyme
- 1/2tsp Pepper

DIRECTIONS

1. Add all ingredients to a gallon sized baggie or Tupperware and mix to evenly distribute seasoning on the chicken.
2. Refrigerate 30min-1hr to marinate.
3. Heat and lightly oil grill to med/high heat or heat and lightly oil a skillet.
4. Optional- Add hickory wood chips to grill for a smokey flavor.
5. Grill chicken 10min each side (depending on how thick your chicken breasts are, you can flip and cook 5-10min on each side) until golden brown and internal temp is 165.
6. If cooking in a skillet, cover skillet while chicken is cooking.

SINGLE SERVING SIZE-
   4oz = full protein

Weight loss Recipes
- no sugar, no flour, made deliciously easy -
WeightLossRecipesCookbook.com

Air Fryer Roasted Chickpeas

servings: -   cooking time: 8hrs 30min

INGREDIENTS

- 1lb Dried chickpeas
- 6-8cups water
- Spray olive oil

DIRECTIONS

1. Add chickpeas and water to a large bowl and soak 6-8hrs or overnight or use canned chickpeas.
2. Drain and rinse.
3. Pour enough beans to cover the bottom of the air fryer with 1 layer of beans.
4. Spray with olive oil and lightly toss to coat.
5. Fry at 390 for 30min stirring occasionally or until desired consistency.
6. Or roast in the oven 375 for 35-45min stirring occasionally until crispy

SINGLE SERVING SIZE-
    2oz = full protein

Weight loss Recipes
- no sugar, no flour, made deliciously easy -
WeightLossRecipesCookbook.com

Sea Salt Vinegar Air Fried Chickpeas

servings: -   cooking time: 8hrs 30min

INGREDIENTS

- 1lb Dried chickpeas
- 6-8cups water
- Spray olive oil
- 1Tbsp White vinegar
- 1/2tsp Sea salt

DIRECTIONS

1. Add chickpeas and water to a large bowl and soak 6-8hrs or overnight or use canned chickpeas.
2. Drain and rinse.
3. Pat dry with a towel.
4. Add chickpeas, vinegar, and salt to a large bowl.
5. Spray beans with olive oil and toss to combine.
6. Pour enough beans to cover the bottom of the air fryer with 1 layer of beans.
7. Spray with olive oil.
8. Fry at 390 for 30min stirring occasionally or until desired consistency.
9. Or roast in the oven 375 for 35-45min stirring occasionally until crispy

SINGLE SERVING SIZE-
2oz = full protein

Weight loss Recipes
- no sugar, no flour, made deliciously easy -
WeightLossRecipesCookbook.com

Chipotle Air Fried Chickpeas

servings: -   cooking time: 8hrs 30min

INGREDIENTS

- 1lb Dried chickpeas
- 6-8cups water
- Spray olive oil
- 1/4tsp of each: Sea salt, chipotle pepper powder
- 1/2tsp of each: Chili powder, garlic powder

DIRECTIONS

1. Add chickpeas and water to a large bowl and soak 6-8hrs or overnight or use canned chickpeas.
2. Drain and rinse.
3. Pat dry with a towel.
4. Add chickpeas and seasonings to a large bowl.
5. Spray beans with olive oil and toss to combine.
6. Pour enough beans to cover the bottom of the air fryer with 1 layer of beans.
7. Spray with olive oil.
8. Fry at 390 for 30min stirring occasionally or until desired consistency.
9. Or roast in the oven 375 for 35-45min stirring occasionally until crispy

SINGLE SERVING SIZE-
2oz = full protein

Weight loss Recipes
- no sugar, no flour, made deliciously easy -
WeightLossRecipesCookbook.com

2 Ingredient Lentil Tortillas

servings: -   cooking time: 3min

INGREDIENTS

- 1lb Dried lentils
- 4 1/2cups Water
- 6 cups Water
- Pinch of salt

DIRECTIONS

1. Add lentils and 6 cups water to a large bowl.
2. Let soak 4-6hrs or overnight.
3. Drain and rinse.
4. Add lentils, salt, and 4 1/2cups water to a blender and blend on high until smooth.
5. Heat and lightly oil a skillet on med/low heat.
6. Add 1/4cup batter to skillet and spread thin with a spoon.
7. Cook 1-2min, flip and cook 1 min longer.
8. Repeat with remaining batter.
9. You may need to re-oil pan if tortillas start to stick.

SINGLE SERVING SIZE-

1 1/2oz tortilla = ¼ protein,
3oz tortillas = ½ protein,
6oz tortilla = full protein

Weight loss Recipes
- no sugar, no flour, made deliciously easy -
WeightLossRecipesCookbook.com

Lentil Flatbread

servings: -   cooking time- 25min

INGREDIENTS

- 1lb Raw lentils
- 6cups Water

DIRECTIONS

1. Add water to a pot and bring to a boil.
2. Rinse lentils.
3. Add lentils to boiling pot, reduce heat to simmer and cover.
4. Simmer 15-20min or until lentils are tender.
5. Do not drain.
6. Using an immersion blender or blender, blend lentils until smooth.
7. Heat and lightly oil a griddle or skillet.
8. Pour 1/4cup of mixture onto griddle and gently poke and spread mixture as thin as you can without creating holes.
9. Cook 4-5min, flip and repeat with remaining mixture.

SINGLE SERVING SIZE-
6oz lentil flatbread = a full protein

Weight loss Recipes
- no sugar, no flour, made deliciously easy -
WeightLossRecipesCookbook.com

Lentil Flatbread Crisps

servings: -   cooking time- 60min

INGREDIENTS

- 1lb Raw lentils
- 6cups Water
- 1Tbsp Chipotle seasoning or season fry seasoning (find seasoning recipes in "Sauces, Seasonings, and Sides")
- Pinch of Everything But The Bagel Seasoning

SINGLE SERVING SIZE-
6oz Lentil flatbread crisps = a full protein

DIRECTIONS

1. Add water to a pot and bring to a boil.
2. Rinse lentils.
3. Add lentils to boiling pot, reduce heat to simmer and cover.
4. Simmer 15-20min or until lentils are tender.
5. Do not drain.
6. Using an immersion blender or blender, blend lentils until smooth.
7. Preheat oven to 380.
8. Line a baking pan with parchment paper.
9. Add 2 cups of blended lentils and chipotle seasoning to a bowl and mix.
10. Spread mixture onto lined pan and sprinkle with Everything But The Bagel Seasoning.
11. Bake 30-40min or until lentils are golden brown and starting to crack.
12. Break into pieces.

Weight Loss Recipes
- no sugar, no flour, made deliciously easy -
WeightLossRecipesCookbook.com

Ginger Cumin Chicken

servings: -   cooking time- 10min

INGREDIENTS

- 1Tbsp Toasted sesame oil
- 5 Raw chicken breasts
- 1/2tsp of each: Ginger, curry powder, ginger, sea salt
- 1tsp of each: Onion powder, garlic powder

DIRECTIONS

1. Thaw chicken.
2. Add seasonings and oil to a large bowl.
3. Add thawed chicken to bowl and toss to coat.
4. Let sit 10-15min to marinate.
5. Heat and lightly oil a skillet over med-high heat.
6. Add chicken and sear each side 1min.
7. Reduce heat to med-low, cover and cook 6-9min or until internal temp reaches 170.
8. Flip halfway for even cooking.

SINGLE SERVING SIZE-
   4oz = full protein

Chili Lime Chicken

servings: -   cooking time- 20min

INGREDIENTS

- 6 Chicken breast
- 1 Green pepper
- 1 Onion
- 1 1/2tsp Chili powder
- 1/3cup Lime juice
- 1tsp of each: Cumin, onion powder, sea salt
- Pinch of Black pepper
- 6-7 Cloves garlic

DIRECTIONS

1. Add thawed chicken breast to a pressure cooker.
2. Dice garlic.
3. Drizzle with lime juice, garlic, and spices.
4. Rub mixture into chicken to coat breasts.
5. Slice peppers and onion.
6. Place peppers and onions on top.
7. Pressure cook on high 10min, natural release 5min then quick release or bake 350 for 1hr 30min or until internal temp is 160.
8. Remove chicken and shred using 2 forks
9. Add chicken back to juice and stir to prevent chicken drying out.

SINGLE SERVING SIZE–
    4oz = full protein

Weight loss Recipes
- no sugar, no flour, made deliciously easy -
WeightLossRecipesCookbook.com

111

Pressure Cooker Seasoned Chicken

servings: -   cooking time- 23min

INGREDIENTS

- 1tsp of each: Paprika, parsley, basil, rosemary, garlic powder
- 1/2tsp Sea salt
- 5 Chicken breast
- 1cup Vegetable broth

DIRECTIONS

1. Turn on sauté setting on the pressure cooker and lightly oil.
2. Mix seasonings in a bowl.
3. Sprinkle and rub seasoning into chicken breasts.
4. Sear chicken 2-3min each side.
5. Remove chicken, add broth and trivet to pressure cooker.
6. Add chicken to pressure cooker.
7. Close lid and pressure cook on high 10min.
8. Natural release 10min before quick release.
9. Make sure chicken internal temperature is at least 160.

SINGLE SERVING SIZE-
4oz = full protein

Weight loss Recipes
- no sugar, no flour, made deliciously easy -
WeightLossRecipesCookbook.com

Savory Lentil Wraps

servings: -   cooking time- 5min

INGREDIENTS

- 3cups Uncooked lentils
- 6cups water
- 2tsp of each: Garlic salt, baking soda
- 2Tbsp Garlic powder

DIRECTIONS

1. Add lentils and water to a large bowl.
2. Soak 4hrs-overnight.
3. Drain and rinse lentils.
4. Add lentils, spices, and another 6cups of water to a blender.
5. Blend until smooth.
6. Heat and lightly oil a skillet over medium heat.
7. Pour 1/3cup of lentil batter into skillet and cook 2-3min.
8. Flip and cook another 1-2min.
9. Repeat with remaining batter.

SINGLE SERVING SIZE–
3oz lentil wraps = ½ protein
6oz lentil wrap = full protein

Weight loss Recipes
- no sugar, no flour, made deliciously easy -
WeightLossRecipesCookbook.com

Sweet Lentil Wraps

servings: -   cooking time- 5min

INGREDIENTS

- 3cups Uncooked lentils
- 6cups Water
- 2tsp of each: Nutmeg, baking soda
- 2Tbsp of each: Vanilla extract, cinnamon
- Pinch of Sea salt

DIRECTIONS

1. Add lentils and water to a large bowl.
2. Soak 4hrs-overnight.
3. Drain and rinse lentils.
4. Add lentils, spices, and another 6cups of water to a blender.
5. Blend until smooth.
6. Heat and lightly oil a skillet over medium heat.
7. Pour 1/3cup of lentil batter into skillet and cook 2-3min.
8. Flip and cook another 1-2min.
9. Repeat with remaining batter.

SINGLE SERVING SIZE-
3oz lentil wraps = ½ protein
6oz lentil wrap = full protein

Weight loss Recipes
- no sugar, no flour, made deliciously easy -
WeightLossRecipesCookbook.com

Lentil Pizzelle

servings: -   cooking time- 30sec

INGREDIENTS

- 1cup Dried lentils
- 5cups Water
- 1tsp Baking soda
- Pinch Sea salt

DIRECTIONS

1. Rinse and soak lentils in 4 cups of water 3hrs-overnight.
2. Drain water from lentils.
3. Using a high-powered blender add soaked lentils, 1 cup water, baking soda, and salt.
4. Blend until smooth.
5. Heat and lightly oil a pizzelle maker or lightly oil a skillet.
6. Scoop 1Tbsp of batter into each pizzelle mold and cook 30sec.
7. Repeat with remaining batter.

SINGLE SERVING SIZE-
6oz = full protein

Weight loss Recipes
- no sugar, no flour, made deliciously easy -
WeightLossRecipesCookbook.com

Oriental Chicken

servings: -   cooking time- 30min

INGREDIENTS

- 2lbs Chicken breast
- 1/4cup Apple cider vinegar
- 3/4cup Soy sauce
- 1Tbsp of each: Oriental seasoning, minced garlic, nutritional yeast

DIRECTIONS

1. Dice raw chicken into small cubes.
2. Add all ingredients to a large saucepan/skillet and stir.
3. Let sit 10-15min to marinate.
4. Heat saucepan to high heat until starting to sizzle.
5. Reduce heat to med/high cover and cook 10-15min stirring occasionally.
6. Remove cover and reduce heat to medium.
7. Simmer until all liquid is absorbed.
8. Using 2 forks lightly shred chicken.

SINGLE SERVING SIZE-
    4oz = full protein

Weight loss Recipes
- no sugar, no flour, made deliciously easy -
WeightLossRecipesCookbook.com

Marinated Tuna Steak

servings: -   cooking time- 40min

INGREDIENTS

- Tuna Steak
- Olive oil
- Sea salt
- Paprika
- Onion powder
- Garlic powder
- Parsley
- Basil

DIRECTIONS

1. Place tuna steaks in a large Tupperware and drizzle with olive oil and sprinkle with seasonings.
2. Refrigerate 30min-4hrs or longer. Shake ever so often to distribute the marinade
3. Heat and lightly oil a skillet.
4. Add tuna steaks to skillet and sprinkle with more seasonings
5. Cook 3-4minn or until bottom starts to turn white, then it is ready to flip.
6. Cook another 3-4min or until your desired doneness.

SINGLE SERVING SIZE-
   4oz = full protein

Weight loss Recipes
- no sugar, no flour, made deliciously easy -
WeightLossRecipesCookbook.com

Grilled Pesto Chicken

servings: -   cooking time- 30min

INGREDIENTS

- Raw chicken breast
- Fat free pesto (find pesto recipe in "Sauces, Seasonings, and Sides")
- Sea salt
- Spray olive oil

DIRECTIONS

1. Heat grill to medium/high heat.
2. Spray chicken breast with olive oil and sprinkle with salt.
3. Grill chicken 10-15min each side.
4. Brush/rub chicken with pesto and grill 5min each side.
5. Cook until internal temp reaches 160.

SINGLE SERVING SIZE-
4oz = full protein

Weight loss Recipes
- no sugar, no flour, made deliciously easy -
WeightLossRecipesCookbook.com

Fat Free Hummus

servings: -   cooking time- 30min

INGREDIENTS

- 1 Can Chickpeas
- 1/4cup of each: Aquafaba (liquid from can of chickpeas), spaghetti sauce
- Pinch of each: Garlic salt, onion powder, paprika, sea salt
- 2Tbsp Lemon juice
- 3/4tsp Cumin
- 1 Clove garlic

DIRECTIONS

1. Add all ingredients to a food processor and blend until smooth.
2. If mixture is to thick add a little more spaghetti sauce to thin.

SINGLE SERVING SIZE-
6oz = full protein

Find this recipe also in my Volume 10, Cooking with Joy 2, and the Whole Food Plant Based, Vegan volume 2 cookbooks

Weight loss Recipes
- no sugar, no flour, made deliciously easy -
WeightLossRecipesCookbook.com

Golden Hummus

servings: -   cooking time-

INGREDIENTS

- 1 Can chickpeas
- 3Tbsp of each: Lemon juice, tahini
- 2 Cloves garlic
- 1tsp Ginger
- 1/2tsp Turmeric
- 1/4tsp Sea salt
- 1Tbsp Olive oil
- Water

DIRECTIONS

1. Add all ingredients except water to a food processor.
2. Process until smooth.
3. Add water until desired consistency.

SINGLE SERVING SIZE-
6oz = full protein

Find this recipe also in my Volume 11, Cooking with Joy 2, and the Whole Food Plant Based, Vegan volume 2 cookbooks

Weight loss Recipes
- no sugar, no flour, made deliciously easy -
WeightLossRecipesCookbook.com

Pesto Hummus

servings: -   cooking time-

INGREDIENTS

- 1 can Chickpeas
- 1/2oz Fresh basil leaves
- 1Tbsp of each: Olive oil, tahini
- Pinch of Sea salt
- 1/2oz Lemon juice
- 2 cloves Garlic

DIRECTIONS

1. Add all ingredients to a food processor or use a hand blender and blend until smooth.

SINGLE SERVING SIZE-
  4oz = a full protein
    2oz = full fat

Find this recipe also in my
Volume 12 and Cooking with Joy
2 cookbooks

Sauces, Seasonings, and Sides

PARTY SERVINGS

Weight loss Recipes
- no sugar, no flour, made deliciously easy -
WeightLossRecipesCookbook.com

Peanut Asian Noodle Salad

servings: 30-50   cooking time: -

INGREDIENTS

- 1 Red pepper
- 1 Yellow pepper
- 2 Small red onions
- 2 12oz Bag angel hair cabbage
- 2 Small bags Sugar snap peas
- 1 Small can Mushrooms
- 1 Small can Water chestnuts
- 1 Bunch Green onion
- 2 Cans Palmini pasta
- 2 Cans Chickpeas
- 1/2 16oz Container Crunchy peanut butter
- 3Tbsp of each: G Hughes Sugar Free Orange Ginger Marinade, soy sauce, apple cider vinegar, toasted sesame oil
- 2tsp of each: Garlic powder, onion powder, ginger, everything but the bagel seasoning
- 1Tbsp Minced garlic
- 1/4cup water

DIRECTIONS

1. Slice and dice vegetables.
2. Drain chestnuts, mushrooms, and palmini noodles.
3. Add all vegetables to a large bowl.
4. Drain chickpeas and add to bowl.
5. In a separate bowl mix seasonings, sauces, minced garlic, and water.
6. Pour sauce mixture onto vegetables and toss/mix

SINGLE SERVING SIZE- 6 OR 14OZ TOTAL VEGETABLES

1/2oz Toasted sesame oil, 3oz Chickpeas, 1oz Peanut butter, 1Tbsp of each: G Hughes Sugar Free Orange Ginger Marinade, soy sauce, apple cider vinegar, toasted sesame oil. 4Tbsp water, 2tsp Minced garlic, 1/2tsp of seasonings

Weight loss Recipes
- no sugar, no flour, made deliciously easy -
WeightLossRecipesCookbook.com

Party Peanut Butter Frosted Apple Crisp

servings: 30   cooking time: 50min

INGREDIENTS

- 10 Apples
- 3 Bananas
- 1 32oz Plain Greek yogurt
- 2 16oz Crunchy peanut butter
- 2Tbsp of each: Instant coffee, cinnamon, apple pie spice, maple extract (find seasoning recipe in "Sauces, Seasonings, and Sides")
- 3Tbsp Lemon juice
- Pinch of Sea salt
- 2 Cans chickpeas

SINGLE SERVING SIZE-
11 1/2oz = full protein, fruit, and fat.

DIRECTIONS

1. Preheat oven to 375.
2. Dice apples and add to a large cake pan or 2 9x13 cake pans.
3. Drizzle with lemon juice.
4. Sprinkle apples with cinnamon, instant coffee, and salt.
5. Drain and blend chickpeas with a hand blender or food processor.
6. Add bananas, 1 container peanut butter, remaining seasonings, to chickpeas and mash/mix.
7. Sprinkle chickpea mixture on top of apples and bake 45-50min.
8. Add remaining peanut butter and yogurt to a large baggie and mash/mix.
9. Cut corner of baggie and pipe mixture into crisp.

Weight loss Recipes
- no sugar, no flour, made deliciously easy -
WeightLossRecipesCookbook.com

4th of July Party Salad

servings: -   cooking time-

INGREDIENTS

- 5 Large cucumbers
- 1 Purple cabbage
- 2 Red onion
- 1 Green pepper
- 1 12oz bag Shredded carrots
- 2 Roma tomatoes
- 1cup Lemon juice
- 1/2cup Apple cider vinegar
- 1tsp Garlic salt
- 1Tbsp of each: Dijon mustard, basil, parsley
- 2tsp Onion powder
- Pinch of Sea salt

DIRECTIONS

1. Dice all vegetables into small pieces.
2. Add vegetables to a large bowl and mix.
3. In a separate bowl, whisk seasonings, lemon juice, vinegar, and Dijon.
4. Pour mixture onto salad and mix.
5. Refrigerate 30min-overnight for best flavor.

SINGLE SERVING SIZE-
6oz = full lunch vegetables
14oz = full dinner vegetables

Weight loss Recipes
- no sugar, no flour, made deliciously easy -
WeightLossRecipesCookbook.com

Cheesecake Berry Salad

servings: 30-50   cooking time-

INGREDIENTS

- 3 32oz Plain Greek yogurt
- 3 12oz Container whipped cream cheese or regular cream cheese
- 6-8 Bananas
- 1 12oz Bag frozen mixed berries
- 1 2lb Bag frozen mixed berries
- 1/3cup Lemon juice
- 1/2tsp Sea salt
- 2tsp Vanilla extract
- Pinch of Cinnamon

DIRECTIONS

1. Mash banana, cream cheese, vanilla, salt, and lemon juice.
2. Add yogurt and mix.
3. Fold in 2lb bag of frozen berries.
4. Sprinkle with cinnamon and top with 12oz bag of berries.
5. Serve right away or refrigerate overnight for best flavor.

SINGLE SERVING SIZE-
12oz = full fruit, protein, and fat.
Side with 6oz vegetables for a complete lunch

Sauces, Seasonings, and Sides

SEASONINGS

Weight Loss Recipes
- no sugar, no flour, made deliciously easy -
WeightLossRecipesCookbook.com

185

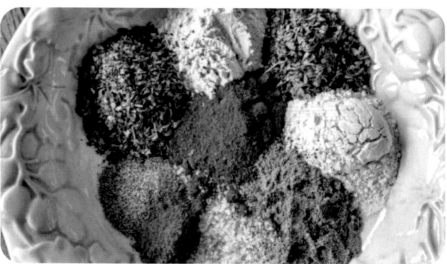

Chipotle Seasoning

servings: -   cooking time: -

INGREDIENTS

- 1Tbsp of each: Onion powder, parsley, basil, garlic powder
- 1/2Tbsp Cumin
- 2tsp Chipotle pepper powder
- 1tsp of each: Sea salt, black pepper
- 1/2tsp Cayenne pepper

DIRECTIONS

Add all ingredients to a spice container and mix.

Weight loss Recipes
- no sugar, no flour, made deliciously easy -
WeightLossRecipesCookbook.com

Gingerbread spice

servings: -   cooking time: -

INGREDIENTS

- 3Tbsp of each: Ground Ginger, cinnamon
- 1tsp of each: Allspice, nutmeg
- 3/4 tsp Cardamom
- 1/2 tsp Cloves

DIRECTIONS

1. Add all ingredients to a spice container and mix.

Weight loss Recipes
- no sugar, no flour, made deliciously easy -
WeightLossRecipesCookbook.com

187

Ranch Seasoning

servings: -   cooking time- -

INGREDIENTS

- 2Tbsp Dill
- 2tsp of each: Garlic powder, onion powder, parsley
- 1tsp of each: Garlic salt, basil

DIRECTIONS

1. Add all ingredients to a spice container.
2. Mix

Weight loss Recipes
- no sugar, no flour, made deliciously easy -
WeightLossRecipesCookbook.com

Oriental Seasoning

servings: -   cooking time-

INGREDIENTS

- 2Tbsp of each Garlic powder, ginger, onion powder
- 2tsp of each: Sea salt, pepper

DIRECTIONS

1. Add all ingredients to a spice container.
2. Shake/mix

Weight loss Recipes
- no sugar, no flour, made deliciously easy -
WeightLossRecipesCookbook.com

Pumpkin Pie Spice

servings: -   cooking time-

INGREDIENTS

- 3Tbsp Cinnamon
- 2tsp of each: Ginger, nutmeg
- 1tsp of each: Allspice, cloves

DIRECTIONS

1. Add all ingredients to a spice container.
2. Shake/mix

Weight loss Recipes
- no sugar, no flour, made deliciously easy -
WeightLossRecipesCookbook.com

Apple Pie Spice

servings: -   cooking time-

INGREDIENTS

- 4Tbsp Cinnamon
- 1 1/2tsp of each: Nutmeg, cardamon
- 1tsp Ginger
- 1/2tsp Allspice

DIRECTIONS

1. Add all ingredients to a spice container.
2. Shake/mix

Greek Spice Blend

servings: -   cooking time-

INGREDIENTS

- 1Tbsp of each: Garlic powder, basil, oregano
- 1 1/2tsp of each: Sea salt, pepper, parsley, rosemary, thyme
- 3/4tsp Nutmeg

DIRECTIONS

1. Add all ingredients to a spice container.
2. Shake/mix

192

Weight loss Recipes
- no sugar, no flour, made deliciously easy -
WeightLossRecipesCookbook.com

Latte Spice

servings: -   cooking time-

INGREDIENTS

- 3Tbsp Cinnamon
- 1Tbsp Instant coffee
- 1 1/2Tbsp of each: Nutmeg, cardamon
- 1/4tsp Sea salt

DIRECTIONS

1. Add all ingredients to a spice container.
2. Shake/mix

Chai spice

servings: -   cooking time-

INGREDIENTS

- 2tsp of each: Cardamom, allspice, nutmeg, cloves
- 4tsp Cinnamon
- 6tsp Ginger

DIRECTIONS

1. Add all ingredients to a spice container.
2. Shake/mix

FIND THIS RECIPE ALSO IN MY VOLUME 9 COOKBOOK AND COOKING WITH JOY

Weight loss Recipes
- no sugar, no flour, made deliciously easy -
WeightLossRecipesCookbook.com

Hash Seasoning

servings: -   cooking time-

INGREDIENTS

- 1Tbsp of each: Paprika, garlic powder
- 1/2Tbsp of each: Sea salt, pepper, onion powder
- 1tsp of each: Cayenne powder, cumin, turmeric
- 2tsp of each: Oregano, thyme

DIRECTIONS

1. Add all ingredients to a spice container.
2. Shake/mix

**FIND THIS RECIPE
ALSO IN MY VOLUME 4
COOKBOOK AND
COOKING WITH JOY**

Weight loss Recipes
- no sugar, no flour, made deliciously easy -
WeightLossRecipesCookbook.com

195

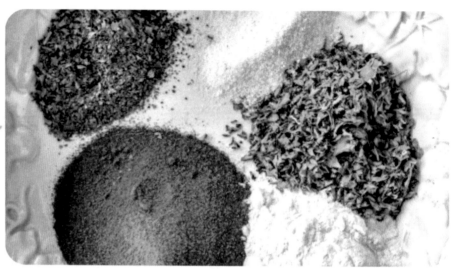

Seasoned Fry Spice

servings: -   cooking time-

INGREDIENTS

- 2Tbsp of each: Garlic powder, onion powder, parsley
- 2 1/2Tbsp Paprika
- 2tsp Garlic salt

DIRECTIONS

1. Add all ingredients to a spice container.
2. Shake/mix

FIND THIS RECIPE ALSO IN MY VOLUME 13 COOKBOOK

Weight loss Recipes
- no sugar, no flour, made deliciously easy -
WeightLossRecipesCookbook.com

Taco Seasoning

servings: -   cooking time-

INGREDIENTS

- 1cup Chili powder.
- 4tsp of each: Garlic powder, onion powder, crushed red pepper flakes, dried oregano
- 8tsp Paprika
- ½cup Cumin
- 1Tbsp of each: Sea salt, pepper

DIRECTIONS

1. Add all ingredients to a spice container.
2. Shake/mix
3. Use 1Tbsp per 1lb of meat

FIND THIS RECIPE ALSO IN MY VOLUME 1 COOKBOOK

About the Author

Find all of my cookbooks, video's, recipes, recipe index, food galleries, and more on my website WeightLossRecipesCookbook.com

Weight loss Recipes
- no sugar, no flour, made deliciously easy -
WeightLossRecipesCookbook.com

Natalie Aul

Picture from left to right. Tom-dad, Kelly-older sister, Maggie-mom, John, older brother, Natalie-me

Natalie was born and raised in Minnesota and was home-schooled along with her siblings. She works full-time with her family at Love of God Family Church in Fergus Falls, Minnesota, leading worship, singing, playing keyboard, and drums. She also writes skits and performs with the church's Blast Kids program.

A little about me.

Growing up I never knew how normal healthy people ate. I have been overweight since I was about 9 years old. I always felt insecure about my weight and eating around others. Then as a family, we changed our diets to whole, healthy foods... and I still was overweight (it is possible to eat healthy foods and still be overweight). We never gave up our Friday night junk foods though... Which slowly grew into Friday, Saturday junk food... Then into all weekend junk foods... And cravings all the rest of the week

As I grew up, I tried all the different kinds of diets with my mom and sister. They never lasted. The sugar and flour were always there... just waiting for us to fail... and we did. I even tried the keto diet and lost 10 pounds! But...I went right back to the old eating habits.

Until one day, my mom called my sister and I into her room. She showed us the first video to an amazing plan on Facebook. It talked about how this way of eating takes all the willpower out. (Which is what we needed!!)We three girls started and went all out. Once we started, we quickly found out that this is the best lifestyle-ever!

For a couple of years, God had been speaking to my mom and He told her, "Your influence for Me will not be as effective in society if you remain overweight. People will be more accepting and open if you will lose the weight." (Sadly, our society is very judgmental) So that's what we did. This has been the best lifestyle change. (it is not a diet). I have lost over 87lbs and have never felt better! The body insecurities are GONE! I don't have to think, "What are they thinking about me. Do I look fat?

After

Will I fit in that chair? I have to shop in the plus size section while all of my friends get to shop in the cute clothing sections." Now I can just throw on jeans and a t-shirt and I don't have to worry about my body or what I look like. I have so much energy. I don't have the tired headaches or the 'blec' feeling after eating junk food. I never have to feel insecure about eating food in front of other people. I can shop in the normal size people sections. I have never been this skinny in my whole life and I will never go back to the old me. Never! I'm not at my goal weight yet but I'm enjoying the journey. It is truly Deliciously Free!!

With Joy, Natalie

Follow me on
Tiktok
Instagram
Facebook
Youtube
Pinterest
and more!

For daily inspiration,
updates, fun, and more

@ WeightLossRecipesCookbook

Love of God Family Church

Loving God
His Word, His People

It's like coming home...

We're a family growing together in worship. We serve, laugh, play games, learn, and we share one another's victories and sorrows.

Our doors are open. Our hearts are open, also. If you're looking for a place to belong and grow close to God,

Welcome home!

Pastors Tom & Maggie Aul

www.LoveofGodFamilyChurch.com

VIDEO PRODUCTION

Let me help you make affordable, memorable videos that capture life's priceless moments and will last for generations.

- **GRADUATION VIDEOS**
- **WEDDING VIDEOS**
- **MEMORIAL VIDEOS**
- **SLIDESHOWS**
- **VIDEO INTRO / OUTRO**
- **ADVERTISEMENT VIDEOS**
- **VIDEOS LOOPS**
- **INSTRUCTIONAL VIDEOS**
- **VHS TO DVD TRANSFER**

GRAPHIC DESIGNER

Let me help you in all of your advertising needs, whether it's a fun event or a new business venture. I will work with you to create affordable designs that will catch everyone's eye and make a lasting impression.

- **LOGOS**
- **FLYERS**
- **BUSINESS CARDS**
- **NEWSLETTERS**
- **MAGAZINES**
- **BROCHURES**
- **COVER LETTERS**
- **POWERPOINTS**
- **PHOTO EDITING**
- **DVD/CD COVERS**
- **BASIC WEBSITE DESIGNER**
- **FACEBOOK COVER PHOTOS**
- **SOCIAL MEDIA MANAGER**

— PUBLISHER —

Have you written a poem, children's book, or novel but don't know how to share it with the world? Let me help! I will work with you in creating a unique and professional looking book, without it costing a fortune.

- **PUBLISH ON AMAZON BARNES & NOBLE**
- **BOOK COVERS**
- **FORMATTING**
- **EDITING**
- **EBOOKS**
- **PAPERPACK BOOKS**
- **HARDCOVER BOOKS**
- **ISBN NUMBERS**
- **EIN TAX ID NUMBERS**

WHETHER YOU ARE A CHURCH, COMPANY, SMALL BUSINESS, OR WANT TO PUBLISH YOUR WORK, I WOULD LIKE TO HELP YOU, ALL THE WHILE KEEPING IT LOW COST AND AFFORDABLE. I WANT TO MAKE THE ENTIRE PROCESS AS EASY AND SIMPLE AS POSSIBLE. PLEASE CONTACT ME TODAY FOR A CONSULTATION AND QUOTE FOR WHAT YOU ARE LOOKING FOR. I LOOK FORWARD TO HELPING YOU. KELLY

This book was published by Purebooks Publishing Company which is a part of Kelly's Complete Digital Design.

KELLYAULNOVELS.COM

KELLYAULNOVELS.COM
FACEBOOK.COM/ KELLYAULNOVELS

Made in the USA
Middletown, DE
16 September 2023

38615909R00119